The Amazing Adventures of
MR. GRANT MONEY

Dear Reader,

Thank you for embarking on this exciting journey with "The Amazing Adventures of Mr. Grant Money." I'm thrilled to share with you the valuable insights and lessons contained within these pages, lessons that have empowered countless individuals and organizations to achieve remarkable success in their grant acquisition endeavors.

Grant funding is a powerful tool, and this book is designed to be your companion as you navigate the intricate world of grant writing. Within these stories lie not just narratives but essential lessons that will guide you toward securing funding for your projects. As you read and engage with the exercises, I hope you find inspiration and actionable strategies to elevate your grant acquisition efforts to new heights.

Throughout my career, I've had the privilege of assisting many individuals starting from ground zero, witnessing their transformation into successful grant seekers. The stories and lessons in this book encapsulate some of the crucial insights that have contributed to their achievements.

However, I must take a moment to introduce you to another invaluable resource—the "Grant Writing That Gets Funded" training. This training has been a cornerstone in the success stories of numerous students and organizations. Tailored for beginners and intermediate grant professionals, it offers clear and comprehensive guidance. Participants not only absorb my exclusive Grant Writing Success Formula but also leave with a personalized 30-Day Grant Empowerment Strategy and Grant Readiness Resource.

Our training has played a pivotal role in agencies securing substantial funding, ranging from $25,000 to millions, in a remarkably short period. You can witness some of these success stories at WowTheyDidIt.com. I am confident that with our support, you could be the next success story, unlocking a bountiful windfall of grant funding for your endeavors.

Imagine the impact on your team as they gain insights, adopt best practices, and leverage industry secrets, giving your agency a competitive edge. This training could be the pivotal factor that distinguishes you from others, ensuring you secure the grants you pursue.

As Kjeld Linstead, a past participant, expressed, "Thanks again for the grants class a few months ago... Since taking your class, I have landed nearly $4 Million in state and federal grants for the City of Redlands."

For more information about the Grant Writing That Gets Funded training, please visit GrantWritingClasses.org. You can also secure your spot by calling 1-888-293-0284. This investment in your organization's financial stability is a strategic move towards a more prosperous future.

Best Regards,

Rodney
Grant Central USA

P.S. Be sure to try our free grant training at StrategicGrantWriting.com.

The Amazing Adventures of
MR. GRANT MONEY

Grantopoly: Mr. Grant Money's Out-of-This-World Wisdom

VOLUME THREE

RODNEY WALKER

Copyright © 2024, Strive Press LLC

All rights reserved. No part of the material protected by this copyright notice may be reproduced or utilized in any form or by any means, electronic or mechanical, including photocopying, recording, or by any information storage and retrieval system, without permission from the copyright owner.

Under no circumstances will any blame or legal responsibility be held against the publisher or author for any damages, reparation, or monetary loss due to the information contained within this book. Either directly or indirectly. You are responsible for your own choices, actions, and results.

For related titles and support materials, visit our online catalog at www.mrgrantmoney.com and www.grantcentralusa.com

Legal Notice:

This book is copyright-protected. This book is only for personal use. You cannot amend, distribute, sell, use, quote, or paraphrase any part of this book's content without the author's or publisher's consent.

Disclaimer Notice:

Please note the information contained within this document is for educational and entertainment purposes only. All effort has been executed to present accurate, up-to-date, reliable, and complete information. No warranties of any kind are declared or implied. Readers acknowledge that the author is not rendering legal, financial, medical, or professional advice. The content within this book has been derived from various sources. Please consult a licensed professional before attempting any techniques outlined in this book.

By reading this document, the reader agrees that under no circumstances is the author responsible for any losses, direct or indirect, which are incurred as a result of the use of the information contained within this document, including, but not limited to, — errors, omissions, or inaccuracies.

Chief Editor: Laine Minerales
Editorial Assistant: Daniel Tuano
Production Supervisor: Joerje Galo
Electronic Composition: Jairus Agoncillo
Photographer: Studio 5404
Executive Marketing Manager: Jimmy Moore

Discover the breadth of our series, encompassing a myriad of crucial topics. Delve into the realms of grant acquisition, college scholarships, entrepreneurship, social impact, philanthropy, and beyond. Unearth a treasure trove of knowledge and empowerment within our diverse collection. Explore the wealth of insights awaiting you across these transformative series.

To inquire about utilizing The Amazing Adventures of Mr. Grant Money books in the classroom, securing licensing, and exploring special pricing for bulk orders, kindly contact us at info@grantcentralusa.com.

ISBN: 978-0-9659275-3-6

Printed in the United States

Dedication

To my dear brother, Chris Walker,
You've been a constant source of laughter, companionship, and understanding. This book is dedicated to you, with admiration for the unique bond we share and the way you've enriched my life. Your support has been invaluable on this journey.

With love and appreciation,
Rodney

PREFACE

The Adventures of Mr. Grant Money: A Journey of Transformation

In the world of grant acquisition, where dreams take flight on the wings of well-crafted proposals, where passion meets purpose, and where communities are transformed through the power of giving, I invite you to embark on a remarkable journey. These adventures are not just a recounting of tales but a testament to the evolution of a grant professional who started with the humblest of beginnings and emerged as a Master Grant Acquisition Specialist.

Over two decades in the making, these stories are a blend of my real-life experiences as a grant professional. They unfold the lessons learned, the challenges faced, and the victories achieved. From the time when I was a novice, wide-eyed and eager to write my first grant proposal, seeking a mere $25,000 for a youth development program, to the present, where I've had the privilege of assisting thousands of individuals and organizations worldwide each year, this journey is one of profound transformation.

It all began with the idea of sharing inspiring tales through a series of blog posts, offering snippets of wisdom and knowledge to those in the world of grants. Yet, as I put pen to paper, these stories took on a life of their own, weaving together to form something magical, something special. What started as a caterpillar of inspiration morphed into a butterfly waiting for you to leap onto its wings and embark on a series of captivating journeys.

This collection is intended to educate and entertain, to offer fresh ideas and insights for seasoned veterans of the grant profession, to guide and inspire newcomers, and perhaps even awaken the curiosity of a young student unaware of the incredible world of grant acquisition.

In this adventure, we'll dive into the core of grant writing, explore the depths of fundraising, and unearth the hidden treasures of effective philanthropy. We'll laugh, we'll learn, and we'll leap beyond the boundaries of the ordinary.

But at the heart of it all, this is a testament to the power of belief. For, as you'll discover, belief is the force that propels dreams into reality. As you journey through these tales, remember one word: BELIEVE!

Now, dear reader, join me as we venture forth into the world of Mr. Grant Money's adventures. Let's explore, learn, and transform together. The journey begins with a single page, and the possibilities are endless.

TABLE OF CONTENT

Introduction	8
Beyond Boundaries: Mr. Grant Money's Extraterrestrial Grant Revelation	9
Facing the Funding Wolves: Mr. Grant Money's Alaska Adventure	15
The High-Stakes Lesson: Mr. Grant Money's Poker Wisdom	21
The Texan Diplomat: Mr. Grant Money's Rodeo of Collaboration	28
From Singapore to Oklahoma: Mr. Grant Money's Global Impact	34
White Suit of Wisdom: Mr. Grant Money at the Crystal Waters Championship	40
Unlocking the Seven Keys to Grant Success in a Changing World	45
Secrets of the Grant Whisperer: Mr. Grant Money's Monte Carlo Coup	52
Winning the Grantopoly Game: Mr. Grant Money's San Diego Saga	58
Granting the Impossible: Mr. Grant Money's Celestial Revelation	64
Afterward	69
About the Author	70
Boost Your Grant Game: Additional Resources	71

INTRODUCTION

Greetings, dear readers, and welcome to another captivating volume of Mr. Grant Money's incredible adventures. In "Grantopoly: Mr. Grant Money's Out-of-This-World Wisdom," we invite you to embark on a journey like no other, one that will take you beyond the boundaries of conventional grant acquisition and into uncharted territories of wisdom and creativity.

Within these stories, you'll accompany Mr. Grant Money on adventures that transcend time, space, and even the limits of our imagination. As you join him in overcoming funding challenges and unlocking the secrets of grant success, you'll discover an array of practical lessons to enhance your grant acquisition skills.

Each of these ten stories, brought to life by Mr. Grant Money's vibrant personality, will provide you with a wealth of inspiration and strategies. After each adventure, you'll have the opportunity to engage in exercises carefully designed to help you implement the same strategies that have served our charismatic hero so well. Discussion questions, powerful quotes, and one BIG Idea will enable you to reflect on each story and apply the lessons to your own grant acquisition journey.

This book is a valuable resource for a wide range of readers, including grant writing instructors, college and university students seeking to understand the intricacies of grants, new grant writers, aspiring grant professionals, fundraisers, grant consultants, nonprofit organizations, executive directors, government agencies, faith-based organizations, and anyone eager to enhance their grant acquisition expertise.

What this book is not is equally important. It is not merely a dry account of grant writing techniques. Instead, it's a thrilling adventure, told through the charismatic voice of Mr. Grant Money, that combines storytelling with practical wisdom. You won't find yourself slogging through pages of jargon; instead, you'll be on the edge of your seat as you accompany Mr. Grant Money on one exhilarating journey after another.

As you delve into these tales, remember the power of exploration, creativity, and a willingness to step outside your comfort zone. Mr. Grant Money has mastered the art of grant acquisition by pushing the boundaries, and these stories will inspire you to do the same.

The power word to keep in mind as you embark on this adventure is "elevate." As you read through the pages of "Grantopoly," elevate your understanding, elevate your skills, and elevate your potential. The grant acquisition world is your playground, and with Mr. Grant Money as your guide, you're bound for a remarkable journey.

Beyond Boundaries: Mr. Grant Money's Extraterrestrial Grant Revelation

Grant-Making Inspiration from an Alien Encounter

As Mr. Grant Money found himself on a spaceship, being examined by beings from a world beyond imagination, he stood there in his signature finely tailored suit, vest, and a classy bow tie that could have graced any formal occasion, even one beyond the confines of Earth. His stylish tan Italian shoes, matching cufflinks, glistening ring, and accessories were all subjected to the curious scrutiny of the alien beings.

The aliens spoke in a language that was utterly indiscernible to Mr. Grant Money, but as one of them touched his belly and whispered something into the very depths of his being, he experienced a sensation that tingled from head to toe. It was as if a lightning bolt of inspiration had struck him, igniting brilliant grant-making ideas that flowed into his mind with astonishing clarity.

New strategies, innovative thoughts, and combinations of ideas surged through his consciousness like a cascade of stars in an alien galaxy. While he couldn't fully comprehend what was happening, he felt a profound sense of calm, as though the encounter with these extraterrestrial beings was a gift beyond measure.

In the blink of an eye, a dazzling array of images flooded Mr. Grant Money's mind. He saw cities, their skylines ablaze with opportunity, government officials and mayors forging new paths, and nonprofit executive directors standing at the forefront of change. Billions of dollars swirled in the cosmic tapestry of his imagination, a testament to the boundless potential that his newfound insight would unlock.

And then, just as mysteriously as it had begun, the encounter concluded. A gentle hand touched Mr. Grant Money, and he was brought back to Earth, or more precisely, Portugal. It was a beautiful airline stewardess, her smile radiating warmth and welcome as she informed him of their arrival.

As Mr. Grant Money stepped off the plane onto the Portuguese soil, he couldn't help but wonder where his ventures would take him next. The mysteries of the universe had bestowed upon him a gift—a wealth of inspiration that he was eager to transform into tangible change for the countless nonprofits, government agencies, and communities he would soon encounter.

With a sense of anticipation and a heart full of gratitude for the unexpected encounter among the stars, Mr. Grant Money embarked on his next adventure, ready to share the cosmic wisdom that had been entrusted to him by beings from worlds beyond our own.

"Inspiration knows no bounds, and sometimes, it descends from the cosmos itself. Just as the stars in the alien galaxy illuminated my mind, so too can we illuminate the path to a brighter future for those in need."

-Mr. Grant Money

Exercise: "Galactic Grant Brainstorming"

This exercise is designed to tap into your creative thinking, inspired by Mr. Grant Money's extraterrestrial encounter, and help you generate innovative grant-making ideas.

Objective:*To encourage "out-of-this-world" thinking, spark creativity, and explore unique perspectives for grant-making opportunities.

Steps:

1. Mindfulness Preparation:
- Find a quiet and comfortable space where you can focus without distractions. Take a few deep breaths and clear your mind. Imagine you're embarking on an imaginative journey to the cosmos.

2. Visual Inspiration:
- To stimulate your creativity, explore images of outer space, alien worlds, and galaxies. You can use resources like NASA's website, astronomy books, or even science fiction illustrations. These visuals will set the stage for your galactic brainstorming.

3. Exploration of the Unknown:
- Take a moment to consider the vastness of space, the mysteries it holds, and the infinite possibilities. Think about how the alien encounter in Mr. Grant Money's story sparked a lightning bolt of inspiration. Challenge yourself to open your mind to unconventional ideas and uncharted territories.

4. Ideation Session:
- With your mind in an exploratory and imaginative state, brainstorm grant-making ideas that are beyond the boundaries of traditional thinking. Don't hold back – let your creativity flow. Consider the following questions:

- If you were to secure a grant from extraterrestrial beings, what type of projects or initiatives would you fund?

- How might you integrate advanced alien knowledge into grant-making strategies?

- What innovative technologies or approaches might be inspired by the encounter with beings from another world?

5. Ideas Galore:
- Write down all the ideas that come to mind. Don't worry about practicality at this stage; the goal is to generate a variety of unique concepts.

6. Concept Refinement:
- Review the list of ideas and select one or more that stand out to you as particularly intriguing or innovative. Consider how these ideas might be adapted or refined for real-world grant-making scenarios.

7. Research and Development:
- For the selected ideas, conduct some preliminary research to see if there are any existing initiatives or emerging technologies that align with your visionary concepts. Explore potential partners or organizations that might be interested in pursuing these ideas.

8. Plan of Action:
- Create a brief plan of action for implementing your visionary grant-making concept. Outline the steps required to bring this concept to life, including potential partners, resources needed, and timelines.

9. Share and Collaborate:
- Engage with colleagues or peers to share your visionary grant-making concept. Seek their input and perspectives on the feasibility and potential impact. Collaborative brainstorming can help refine your ideas.

10. Project Pitch:
- If you feel confident in the feasibility and value of your visionary concept, consider preparing a concise project pitch. This pitch can be used when discussing grant opportunities with potential funders who are open to innovative and imaginative approaches.

11. Continued Exploration:
- Keep your imaginative and creative thinking alive in your regular grant-making activities. Draw inspiration from your galactic brainstorming sessions to encourage fresh perspectives and innovative grant strategies.

By engaging in this exercise, you can tap into the creative thinking inspired by Mr. Grant Money's encounter with extraterrestrial beings and explore grant-making opportunities from a unique perspective. While not all ideas may be practical, this exercise encourages you to think outside the box and consider innovative approaches to grant acquisition and distribution.

Discussion Questions

1. The story takes an unexpected turn as Mr. Grant Money encounters extraterrestrial beings who provide him with a burst of inspiration. How can this experience be interpreted as a metaphor for creativity and innovation in the field of grant acquisition? What might the "cosmic wisdom" represent in the context of grant-making?

2. Mr. Grant Money's encounter with the aliens results in a surge of innovative grant-making ideas. What are some of the challenges and limitations in implementing creative grant-making strategies in the real world? How can grant seekers balance creativity with practicality?

3. The story presents a sense of wonder and gratitude for the unexpected encounter with the extraterrestrial beings. How can this experience be seen as a reminder of the importance of remaining open to new ideas and perspectives in the field of grants and nonprofit work? How can organizations foster a culture of innovation and exploration?

4. Mr. Grant Money's journey takes him to Portugal, leaving us with the anticipation of his next adventure. What can grant seekers and nonprofit organizations learn from his willingness to embrace new experiences and adapt to unexpected circumstances in their pursuit of funding and impact?

5. The story hints at the transformative potential of the cosmic wisdom Mr. Grant Money received. How can grant-making and grant-seeking be seen as a means to bring about profound change on a large scale, and what role can creative and innovative thinking play in achieving these transformative goals?

 Big Idea The "Cosmic Grants" Think Tank"

Taking inspiration from Mr. Grant Money's approach to identifying and addressing reputation issues, launch a unique "Reputation Doctor" consultation service. This service would specialize in diagnosing and prescribing solutions for reputation problems. Just like Mr. Grant Money's unique approach to grant consultation, the "Reputation Doctor" consultants would offer insights, advice, and action plans to individuals and organizations seeking to improve their public image. This creative and specialized consultancy could potentially fill a niche market for those looking to rebuild trust and credibility in today's digital age.

🔍 Word Search

Embark on an otherworldly adventure with Mr. Grant Money as he encounters extraterrestrial beings on a spaceship and receives a cosmic gift of grant-making inspiration. Explore the mysteries of the universe and discover hidden words that reflect the boundless potential and transformative ideas that have taken root in Mr. Grant Money's mind.

In this puzzle, discover the words related to the extraordinary adventures of Mr. Grant Money. Can you find all the hidden words that capture the essence of this remarkable story?

Now, here are the 14 words for the word search puzzle based on the story:

A	A	I	M	A	G	I	N	A	T	I	O	N	M
G	E	S	T	R	A	T	E	G	I	E	S	P	I
R	E	T	N	U	O	C	N	E	T	S	P	R	I
E	V	I	T	A	M	R	O	F	S	N	A	R	T
S	U	N	I	V	E	R	S	E	A	O	I	A	P
V	O	S	T	I	N	N	O	V	A	T	I	V	E
E	S	M	A	O	B	E	I	N	G	S	I	I	S
O	P	P	O	R	T	U	N	I	T	Y	S	E	G
S	M	I	N	T	F	I	G	A	E	E	S	M	N
R	P	P	G	I	S	N	C	O	S	M	I	C	R
S	R	N	I	N	S	P	I	R	A	T	I	O	N
C	P	I	H	S	E	C	A	P	S	C	S	A	T
R	R	I	M	Y	S	T	E	R	I	E	S	A	C
P	O	T	E	N	T	I	A	L	N	T	N	N	T

POTENTIAL
TRANSFORMATIVE
SPACESHIP
ENCOUNTER
BEINGS
MYSTERIES
COSMIC
UNIVERSE
GIFT
INSPIRATION
OPPORTUNITY
IMAGINATION
INNOVATIVE
STRATEGIES

"In the captivating tale of Mr. Grant Money's encounter with extraterrestrial beings, we're reminded that inspiration can come from the most unexpected places. The cosmic gift he received is a testament to the boundless reservoir of creativity that lies within all of us, waiting to be unleashed."

Facing the Funding Wolves: Mr. Grant Money's Alaska Adventure

Grant-Getting Wisdom From the Wilds

In the remote wilderness of Alaska, a stark contrast to the bustling urban landscapes Mr. Grant Money often frequented, he found himself surrounded by a pack of hungry wolves. His attire remained impeccable—a customary black three-piece suit, a white triangle pocket square, a white flower adorning his lapel, topped with a black hat gently tilted to the side. His faithful scepter, though frequently mistaken for a cane, was firmly in his hand.

The alpha male of the wolf pack snarled menacingly, displaying a set of sharp teeth that seemed to suggest Mr. Grant Money was about to become their next feast. But Mr. Grant Money had a plan, and he was anything but your average prey. His calm, cool, and collected demeanor concealed a mind that was always two steps ahead.

As the alpha wolf approached, Mr. Grant Money pulled down his shades, revealing eyes that gleamed with intelligence and a determination that could pierce the most fortified of bank vaults. He understood the nature of predators—they looked for weakness in their prey. But Mr. Grant Money didn't see himself as prey. One of his favorite quotes had always been, "If you ever see me in a fight with a bear, pray for the bear." It was a mindset that had served him well in countless battles, even ones against the natural world.

With a lightning-quick movement, Mr. Grant Money extended his scepter—a seemingly innocuous accessory, but one that concealed a hidden function. With a press of a concealed button, it emitted a high-pitched frequency that disrupted the wolves' senses, sending them into a temporary state of confusion. It was just enough of a distraction for Mr. Grant Money to reach into his pocket and retrieve a canister of pepper spray.

In one swift motion, he unleashed a cloud of stinging mist that engulfed the wolves, causing them to yelp and retreat. Mr. Grant Money had not broken a sweat; instead, he had used his mental ingenuity and resourcefulness to escape the tense situation unscathed.

As he made his way back to safety, Mr. Grant Money couldn't help but reflect on the similarities between his encounter with the wolves and the struggles faced by nonprofit executive directors. To many of them, the relentless pursuit of funding often felt like being surrounded by hungry wolves, ready to devour their agencies.

With a flash of insight that struck him like lightning, Mr. Grant Money knew he had a message to share. He opened his trusted "Gold-Mine Journal" and penned three key insights:

1. Embrace Your Inner Alpha: Just as he had faced down the alpha wolf with unwavering confidence, nonprofit leaders must exude confidence and strength in their pursuit of funding. Confidence can be a powerful deterrent to those who seek to exploit perceived weaknesses.

2. Resourcefulness Is Key: Like his concealed scepter and pepper spray, nonprofit leaders must utilize every resource at their disposal to overcome challenges. Sometimes, the most unexpected tools can be the most effective.

3. Stay Calm, Stay Smart: In the face of adversity, maintaining a calm and collected demeanor is crucial. Panic can lead to poor decision-making. Trust in your abilities and think your way out of tight spots.

As Mr. Grant Money left the wilds of Alaska behind, he carried these insights with him, ready to share them with nonprofit leaders who felt besieged by the relentless wolves of funding challenges. His adventures were not only about securing grants but also about imparting wisdom and inspiring those who sought his guidance on their own journeys to success.

Exercise: "Alpha Leadership and Resourceful Resilience"

This exercise draws inspiration from Mr. Grant Money's Alaska adventure, focusing on building leadership qualities and resourceful resilience.

Objective: To develop leadership skills, confidence, and resourcefulness when facing funding challenges, drawing from the lessons of Mr. Grant Money's encounter with wolves.

Steps:

1. Embrace Your Inner Alpha:
- Find a quiet space to reflect on your role as a nonprofit leader or grant seeker.
- Visualize yourself as the "alpha" in your funding pursuit, exhibiting confidence, strength, and unwavering determination.
- List three specific ways you can boost your confidence and assertiveness in grant-seeking situations.

2. Resourcefulness Toolkit:
- Imagine you are in a situation where resources are limited, much like Mr. Grant Money's creative use of his scepter and pepper spray.
- Create a list of unconventional tools or strategies that you can employ in your grant acquisition journey. These could be overlooked resources or creative approaches you've never considered before.
- Pick one idea from your list and think about how you can apply it to an upcoming grant-seeking situation

3. Stay Calm, Stay Smart:
- Develop a personal "calm and smart" routine or strategy for situations where grant-seeking becomes particularly challenging.
- This routine could include deep breathing exercises, a quick meditation, or even a mantra that reminds you to stay calm and focused.
- Share your routine with a colleague or mentor, and discuss how it can help you make more thoughtful decisions when faced with grant-related challenges.

4. Role-Playing Alpha Leadership:
- Enlist the help of a friend, colleague, or mentor for a role-playing exercise.
- Assume the role of a nonprofit leader seeking a critical grant, and let your partner play the part of a funder or challenging stakeholder.
- Practice exuding confidence, assertiveness, and calm problem-solving in this scenario.
- After the role-play, discuss what worked well and what could be improved to enhance your leadership qualities in grant-seeking situations.

5. Reflect and Implement:
- Take a few minutes at the end of this exercise to reflect on the insights you've gained.
- Identify one specific grant-seeking situation or challenge where you plan to apply the principles of embracing your inner alpha, resourceful resilience, and staying calm and smart.
- Create an action plan for how you will implement these insights in this specific situation.

6. Progress Evaluation:
- As you encounter grant-seeking challenges and opportunities, regularly review your action plan and adjust it based on your experiences.
- Keep a journal to document your progress, challenges faced, and successes achieved by applying the principles learned from Mr. Grant Money's Alaska adventure.

By participating in this exercise, you will develop valuable leadership skills, enhance your confidence, and foster resourceful thinking when navigating the often challenging world of grant acquisition. Emulating Mr. Grant Money's alpha-like determination and resourcefulness will empower you to face funding challenges with resilience and intelligence.

"Just as I turned a seemingly insurmountable situation to my advantage, nonprofit leaders must harness their resourcefulness and creativity to overcome funding obstacles. The most unexpected tools can be the most effective."
- Mr. Grant Money

Discussion Questions

1. The story presents Mr. Grant Money's encounter with the wolf pack as a metaphor for the challenges nonprofit executive directors face in securing funding. How can the lessons he learned from this experience be applied to the real-world struggles of nonprofit organizations in pursuing financial support?

2. Mr. Grant Money's ability to stay calm and collected in a dangerous situation played a crucial role in his escape. How can nonprofit leaders maintain composure and make wise decisions when faced with funding challenges and adversity? What strategies can they use to stay focused and determined in their pursuit of grants?

3. The story emphasizes resourcefulness and utilizing unexpected tools to overcome challenges. In the context of grant-seeking, what are some creative and unconventional approaches that nonprofit organizations can employ to secure funding or build strong relationships with donors and grantmakers?

4. Mr. Grant Money's "Gold-Mine Journal" contains three key insights for nonprofit leaders. How do these insights relate to the broader themes of confidence, resourcefulness, and staying composed in the face of adversity? Can you provide examples of how nonprofit leaders have successfully applied these principles in their work?

5. The story implies that Mr. Grant Money's adventures are not only about securing grants but also about sharing wisdom and inspiring others on their journeys to success. What are the responsibilities of experienced grant acquisition experts and mentors in supporting and guiding emerging nonprofit leaders and organizations in their quest for funding?

 Big Idea "Grant-Ready" Mindfulness Workshops"

Develop a series of mindfulness workshops tailored for nonprofit professionals and grant seekers. Inspired by Mr. Grant Money's calm and collected demeanor, these workshops would focus on teaching individuals how to manage stress, stay focused under pressure, and make well-informed decisions in the fast-paced world of grant acquisition. By incorporating mindfulness practices into their daily routines, nonprofit leaders can harness their inner calm and channel it into successful grant applications.

🔍 Word Search

Join Mr. Grant Money on a wild Alaskan adventure as he faces down a pack of hungry wolves in his signature impeccable attire. Discover the words hidden in the wilderness that reflect the resourcefulness, confidence, and calm determination that define Mr. Grant Money's approach to overcoming challenges.

In this puzzle, discover the words related to the extraordinary adventures of Mr. Grant Money. Can you find all the hidden words that capture the essence of this remarkable story?

Now, here are the 14 words for the word search puzzle based on the story:

R	T	D	D	I	L	H	S	N	I	R	E	T	R
T	I	E	C	N	E	G	I	L	L	E	T	N	I
I	E	T	G	S	P	I	A	I	I	T	Y	C	I
P	R	E	D	A	T	O	R	H	L	P	E	H	I
E	I	R	A	L	P	H	A	N	E	E	R	A	M
I	T	M	N	L	N	S	M	T	E	C	P	L	P
S	M	I	N	D	S	E	T	I	B	S	S	L	E
C	I	N	L	A	Y	S	A	T	T	I	R	E	C
S	E	A	R	R	O	N	R	T	M	P	O	N	C
E	H	T	L	M	T	E	P	N	S	R	T	G	A
L	W	I	C	L	E	S	N	A	E	G	E	E	B
I	I	O	E	E	I	N	S	I	G	H	T	S	L
L	T	N	P	E	S	E	V	L	O	W	M	P	E
T	U	N	S	C	A	T	H	E	D	A	S	N	E

ATTIRE
ALPHA
SENSES
PREDATOR
SCEPTER
IMPECCABLE
CHALLENGES
PREY
UNSCATHED
DETERMINATION
INTELLIGENCE
WOLVES
MINDSET
INSIGHT

"Mr. Grant Money's remarkable encounter with Alaskan wolves serves as a powerful metaphor for the challenges faced by nonprofit leaders in their quest for funding. It's a reminder that resourcefulness, resilience, and self-assuredness can lead to success even in the most daunting situations."

The High-Stakes Lesson: Mr. Grant Money's Poker Wisdom

Unlocking Success by Avoiding Costly Gambles in Grants and Beyond

Mr. Grant Money, ensconced in the luxurious confines of the Skylofts at MGM Grand, reveled in opulence and the finer things in life. For him, the pursuit of excellence and the embrace of luxury had long been a hallmark of his distinguished persona.

After a session of relaxation and a few games of solitaire in his impeccably tailored suit, Mr. Grant Money decided it was time for a shower. He emerged from the bathroom clad in a new, tailor-made black and gray tuxedo, complete with engraved cufflinks bearing the initials MGM (for Mr. Grant Money) and a dazzling white pocket square adorned with a hint of paisley. His signature cologne wafted through the air as he slipped into patent leather shoes that gleamed with every step.

He made his way to the Bentley waiting for him, where his personal driver greeted him with the utmost professionalism. The chauffeur whisked him away to the back entrance of the Bellagio Hotel, where Mr. Grant Money's presence did not go unnoticed. Heads turned, and flirtatious glances were cast his way, but on this particular night, his thoughts were elsewhere.

Inside the Bellagio, he observed a high-stakes poker game in full swing. It didn't take long for Mr. Grant Money's keen eye to spot a player repeatedly making costly mistakes, resulting in significant losses—even by his own standards. Time and again, this player seemed to fall victim to the same pitfalls.

Though Mr. Grant Money was not one to offer unsolicited advice, he couldn't help but reach for his "Gold-Mine Journal" and scribble some notes, cryptic and legible only to himself. The words he wrote contained a powerful thought, one that resonated not only in the world of high-stakes poker but also in the realms of City Managers, Nonprofit Executive Directors, and Professional Fundraisers.

The note read: "In the pursuit of success, learn from your mistakes. Repeating them is a costly gamble that no one can afford."

With that thought etched into his journal, Mr. Grant Money continued to observe the poker game, a silent observer of both fortune and folly, always ready to glean insights and lessons that could be applied to the many facets of his work.

"In the pursuit of success, learn from your mistakes. Repeating them is a costly gamble that no one can afford."

Exercise: "Strategic Learning from Mistakes"

This exercise is inspired by Mr. Grant Money's observation of a poker game and the valuable lesson he noted in his "Gold-Mine Journal."

Objective: To enhance your decision-making and problem-solving skills by actively learning from past mistakes, whether in grant-seeking or other areas of your professional life.

Steps:

1. Reflection on Past Mistakes:
- Take some time to reflect on your past experiences, especially those involving decisions that didn't yield the desired outcomes in your professional life, be it grant-seeking, project management, or other aspects of your work.

2. Identify Key Mistakes:
- Choose a specific mistake or a recurring pattern of errors that you have made in the past.
- Clearly define what went wrong, the consequences, and the context in which it occurred.

3. Analyze and Document:
- Use a journal or digital document to record the following details about the mistake:
- The specific mistake or decision.
- Factors that contributed to the mistake.
- Consequences of the mistake.
- Your emotions or thoughts at the time.
- The context, including stakeholders involved and the situation.
- What you learned from the mistake or what you would do differently.

4. Extraction of Key Insights:
- Examine the patterns or commonalities among the mistakes you've made.
- Look for overarching lessons or insights that can be drawn from these experiences.
- Consider how these insights can be applied to your grant-seeking efforts or other professional challenges.

5. Formulate Actionable Solutions:
- Based on your insights, outline specific actionable steps or strategies that will help you avoid repeating the same mistakes in the future.
- Consider how these strategies can be incorporated into your work processes, decision-making, and planning.

6. Implement the New Approach:
- Begin integrating the new strategies into your work.
- Track your progress and assess whether the changes lead to better results or fewer mistakes.

7. Regular Review:
- Continually review your efforts, especially when facing situations similar to those where past mistakes occurred.
- Adjust your approach as needed to further improve your decision-making and problem-solving skills.

8. Share the Wisdom:
- If you work within a team or collaborate with colleagues, share the lessons you've learned and the strategies you've implemented.
- Encourage open discussions about past mistakes and collective learning.

By participating in this exercise, you'll develop a proactive approach to learning from past mistakes and applying those lessons to your professional life. Just as Mr. Grant Money observed the high-stakes poker game and extracted valuable wisdom, you'll become more adept at identifying areas for improvement and avoiding costly gambles in grant-seeking and beyond.

"Just as in the world of poker, in the pursuit of grants, the costly gamble is repeating your mistakes. It's a game we can't afford to lose."

- Mr. Grant Money

Discussion Questions

1. The story uses the high-stakes poker game as a backdrop to convey a valuable lesson. How can the costly mistakes made by the poker player in the story be related to the challenges and pitfalls that individuals and organizations face in the pursuit of grants and funding? What are some common mistakes to avoid?

2. Mr. Grant Money's note emphasizes the importance of learning from mistakes and avoiding costly gambles. In the context of grant acquisition and nonprofit work, what are some effective strategies for learning from past failures and making informed, successful decisions in the future?

3. The story portrays Mr. Grant Money as a keen observer who is always ready to glean insights and lessons. How can professionals in the field of grant acquisition, fundraising, and nonprofit management develop the skill of keen observation to enhance their effectiveness in securing funding and achieving their mission?

4. Mr. Grant Money's dedication to the pursuit of excellence and luxury is a defining trait. How can this commitment to excellence be applied to the world of grants and nonprofit work, where achieving success often requires attention to detail, professionalism, and continuous improvement?

5. The story suggests that Mr. Grant Money's wisdom extends beyond the realm of poker to various professional arenas, including City Managers, Nonprofit Executive Directors, and Professional Fundraisers. How can the lesson of learning from one's mistakes and avoiding costly gambles be relevant and valuable in these different roles? What are the specific challenges faced by individuals in these professions, and how can the lesson be applied to address those challenges?

 Big Idea "Strategic Decision-Making Seminars"

Develop a series of seminars or workshops focused on decision-making and strategic thinking for professionals across various fields, inspired by Mr. Grant Money's observation of the poker player's repeated costly mistakes. These seminars would help participants learn how to identify and avoid common pitfalls in their decision-making processes. By analyzing case studies from different industries, individuals can gain a deeper understanding of the consequences of repeating errors. This practical knowledge can be applied to their own professional endeavors, minimizing risks and enhancing their chances of success.

🔍 Word Search

Welcome to the 'Excellence & Luxury' Word Search Puzzle! In this word search, we take a glimpse into the world of Mr. Grant Money, a connoisseur of opulence and refinement. Just as Mr. Grant Money seeks the finest things in life, you'll explore a list of words that echo his quest for excellence. From 'Opulence' to 'Cufflinks,' each word in this puzzle resonates with the luxurious experience Mr. Grant Money enjoys. As you seek out these words, you'll dive into a world of sophistication and style.

In this puzzle, discover the words related to the extraordinary adventures of Mr. Grant Money. Can you find all the hidden words that capture the essence of this remarkable story?

Now, here are the 13 words for the word search puzzle based on the story:

R	C	O	E	C	N	E	S	E	R	P	O	R	V
L	P	O	B	E	E	E	W	H	I	S	K	E	D
O	A	O	B	S	C	S	R	N	C	C	O	S	O
F	I	P	F	O	E	T	L	R	Y	N	C	O	T
O	S	U	M	C	P	R	Y	Y	L	U	I	N	D
N	L	L	P	E	L	P	V	C	F	D	U	A	F
P	E	E	F	N	T	L	S	I	T	C	R	T	F
S	Y	N	F	I	C	T	N	T	N	O	L	E	O
E	S	C	C	O	L	O	G	N	E	G	S	D	R
Y	S	E	F	N	L	I	F	O	L	L	Y	A	T
H	I	M	P	E	C	C	A	B	L	Y	S	O	U
E	E	I	S	E	E	E	P	A	T	E	N	T	N
A	N	O	S	R	E	P	B	E	E	E	E	R	E
N	E	I	O	S	K	N	I	L	F	F	U	C	E

COLOGNE
PATENT
PRESENCE
CUFFLINKS
CRYPTIC
IMPECCABLY
FORTUNE
OPULENCE
FOLLY
PAISLEY
OBSERVING
PERSONA
WHISKED
RESONATED

Mr. Grant Money's sharp observation in the world of poker offers a timeless reminder applicable to all aspects of life: **learning from your mistakes is the most valuable skill** one can master on the path to success.

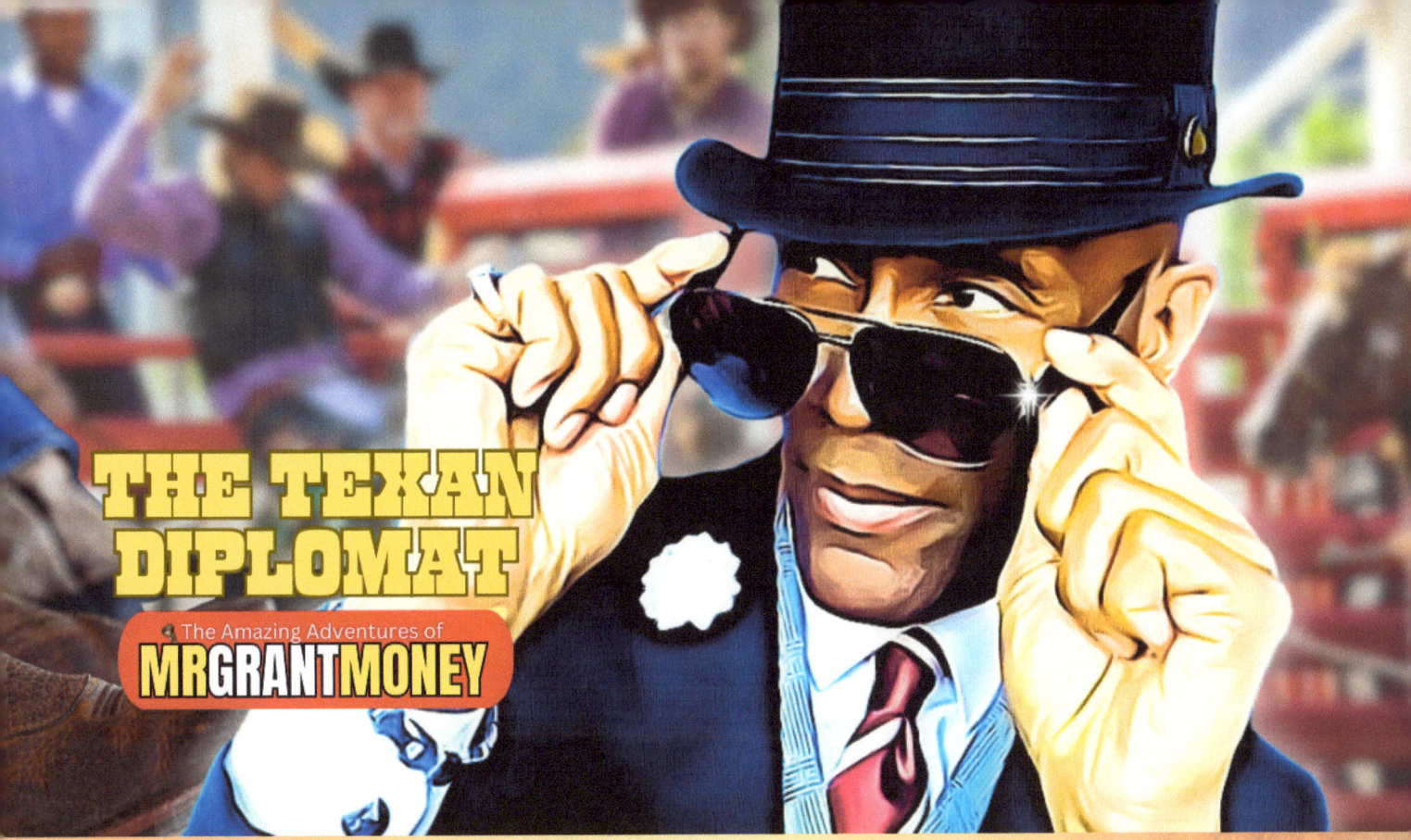

The Texan Diplomat: Mr. Grant Money's Rodeo of Collaboration

Unlocking $247 Million and Uniting Cities for Success

In the vibrant city of Fort Worth, Texas, a historic gathering was taking place. Five mayors from the region had converged to work on a joint effort to secure an impressive $247 million in funding for their communities. It was a rare display of unity and collaboration among leaders, and they were determined to make the most of this opportunity.

As the mayors entered the adjacent conference room, two of them were adorned in classic cowboy hats, reflecting the Texan spirit, while the others brought with them a sense of tradition, each carrying a leather-bound book. They were met with the epitome of elegance in Mr. Grant Money, who was impeccably dressed in a tailored royal blue suit that exuded sophistication. His presence, as always, seemed as if he belonged on the cover of GQ magazine.

Seated at the head of the table, Mr. Grant Money radiated an air of authority and wisdom. To his left sat three mayors, while two occupied seats to his right. By his side was his trusted assistant, Jimmy, who also sported a meticulously tailored light gray suit. The room was an embodiment of high-stakes diplomacy and cooperation.

However, it didn't take long for a less-than-informed comment to slip from the lips of one of the mayors. Jimmy couldn't help but chuckle softly, and Mr. Grant Money, with his characteristic finesse, interjected, "Well, Mayor, that's certainly one way to look at it, but let me offer a perspective that might serve us better in this endeavor."

With grace and charm, Mr. Grant Money proceeded to correct the misinformed comment, providing insights and data to support his perspective. It was a masterful display of tact and diplomacy, and soon, the mayors found themselves aligned with Mr. Grant Money's master plan for securing the $247 million.

After the productive meeting, the group decided to embrace the Texan spirit and headed to the stockyards to enjoy a rodeo. While most attendees at a rodeo were clad in casual attire, Mr. Grant Money, true to his style, attended in his finely tailored suit. He marched to the beat of his own drum, unapologetically himself.

Amidst the excitement of the rodeo, Mr. Grant Money once again reached into his trusted "Gold-Mine Journal" to jot down four key lessons that were important for cities striving to work together:

1. **Embrace Tradition and Innovation**: Just as the mayors blended their Texan tradition with Mr. Grant Money's innovative approach, cities must find a balance between honoring their history and embracing new opportunities.
2. **Tactful Correction**: Diplomacy and tact can correct misconceptions without causing offense. Leaders must be skilled in gently guiding their colleagues towards informed decisions.
3. **Unity is Strength**: Just as the mayors achieved more by working together, cities can accomplish great feats when they collaborate on common goals, setting aside differences for the greater good.
4. **Stay True to Your Style**: Mr. Grant Money's attire at the rodeo was a reminder that one should always remain authentic. Cities should maintain their unique identities while forging collaborations.

With these insights noted, Mr. Grant Money continued his journey to help cities secure funding, one grant at a time, leaving behind a legacy of style, wisdom, and remarkable success.

Exercise: "Synergy and Collaboration for Success"

This exercise is inspired by Mr. Grant Money's successful collaboration with the mayors in Fort Worth, Texas, to secure funding. It aims to foster a spirit of cooperation, effective communication, and innovative thinking in your professional or community endeavors.

Objective: To strengthen collaboration among team members, colleagues, or community leaders by aligning goals, leveraging individual strengths, and working harmoniously toward a common objective.

Steps:

1. Identify Your Collaborative Team:
- Form a group of colleagues or community leaders who share a common goal or project.
- Ensure diversity within the team, as different perspectives can lead to more innovative solutions.

2. Define Your Shared Goal:
- Clearly articulate the shared objective that the team is working toward. It should be specific, measurable, and achievable.

3. Identify Individual Strengths and Resources:
- Have each team member identify their unique strengths, skills, and resources they can contribute to the project.
- Encourage open discussion and self-reflection to uncover these assets.

4. Embrace Tradition and Innovation:
- Discuss how your team can blend traditional and innovative approaches to achieve your goal.
- Identify areas where existing practices can be maintained while integrating new, creative ideas.

5. Tactful Correction and Effective Communication:
- Promote a culture of open communication and constructive feedback within the team.
- Encourage members to respectfully correct misconceptions, provide evidence-based insights, and guide each other towards informed decisions.

6. Unity as a Strength:
- Emphasize the power of unity and collaboration as a driving force for success.
- Discuss instances where teamwork and shared efforts can lead to greater achievements than individual actions.

7. Stay True to Your Style:
- Emphasize the importance of authenticity within the team.
- Encourage members to express their unique perspectives, skills, and approaches while maintaining respect for each other's individuality.

8. Define Roles and Responsibilities:
- Clearly assign roles and responsibilities to each team member based on their strengths and resources.
- Create a plan detailing who will be responsible for specific tasks and milestones.

9. Regular Team Meetings:
- Schedule regular team meetings to review progress, address challenges, and ensure everyone is aligned with the project's goals.
- Use these meetings as opportunities for brainstorming and creative problem-solving.

10. Celebrate Successes:
- Recognize and celebrate achievements, whether they are small milestones or significant accomplishments.
- Use positive reinforcement to motivate and inspire the team.

By engaging in this exercise, you'll foster a collaborative spirit within your team or group, similar to the synergy achieved by the mayors working together with Mr. Grant Money. The exercise emphasizes the value of diversity, effective communication, and a shared vision for success.

Discussion Questions

1. The story highlights the power of collaboration among mayors from different cities in securing $247 million in funding. How can the principles of collaboration, diplomacy, and unity demonstrated in the story be applied to other intergovernmental or interorganizational efforts, and what are the challenges that such collaborations might face?

2. Mr. Grant Money's ability to diplomatically correct a misinformed comment is a key moment in the story. What strategies can leaders use to guide their colleagues or team members toward informed decisions without causing offense or creating conflict, especially in the context of grant acquisition and nonprofit work?

3. The story emphasizes the importance of embracing both tradition and innovation. How can cities and organizations find a balance between honoring their history and culture while also pursuing new opportunities and solutions? What strategies can they employ to maintain a sense of identity while adapting to changing circumstances?

4. Mr. Grant Money's decision to attend the rodeo in his finely tailored suit stands out as an example of staying true to one's style. How can this idea of authenticity and individuality be applied to leadership and decision-making in nonprofit organizations and grant-seeking? What role does authenticity play in building trust and relationships with funders and donors?

5. The story portrays Mr. Grant Money as a successful diplomat and grant acquisition expert. What are the qualities and skills that make Mr. Grant Money an effective leader and collaborator, and how can individuals and organizations in the nonprofit sector develop these qualities to achieve their funding goals and mission?

 Big Idea "Authentic Leadership Style Seminars"

Develop seminars or coaching programs for leaders at all levels, encouraging them to embrace their unique leadership styles. Inspired by Mr. Grant Money's unapologetic authenticity, these seminars would help participants recognize their distinctive qualities and leverage them for success. Leaders would learn how to stay true to their personal style while effectively collaborating with others, thus fostering diversity and unity in leadership.

🔍 Word Search

Dive into the world of city leadership and funding with Mr. Grant Money as he guides five mayors towards securing a substantial $247 million for their communities. Explore the words hidden within the tale, which reflect unity, diplomacy, Texan tradition, and the art of correcting misconceptions with grace.

In this puzzle, discover the words related to the extraordinary adventures of Mr. Grant Money. Can you find all the hidden words that capture the essence of this remarkable story?

Now, here are the 15 words for the word search puzzle based on the story:

ELEGANCE
AUTHENTIC
PERSPECTIVE
LEADERSHIP
IMPECCABLE
DIPLOMACY
INSIGHTS
RODEO
COLLABORATION
MAYORS
AUTHORITY
UNITY
STYLE
TRADITION
FUNDING

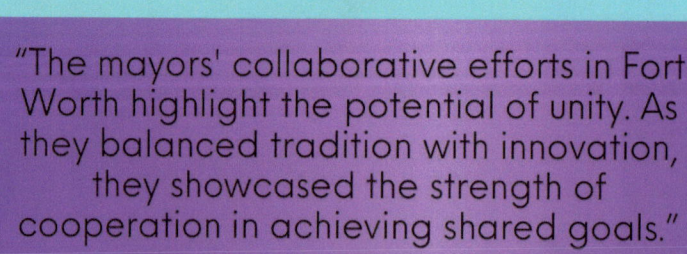

"The mayors' collaborative efforts in Fort Worth highlight the potential of unity. As they balanced tradition with innovation, they showcased the strength of cooperation in achieving shared goals."

From Singapore to Oklahoma: Mr. Grant Money's Global Impact

A Heartfelt Thank-You Card and a $782,000 Transformation

In the heart of the bustling city of Singapore, Mr. Grant Money's attire was, for once, sporty yet still meticulously detailed. His ensemble was a symphony of carefully chosen elements: a tailored navy blazer with a subtle pinstripe pattern, a crisp white shirt complemented by a midnight blue tie, and perfectly fitted khaki trousers.

His signature pocket square, a touch of sophistication, completed the look, and even in this more relaxed attire, every detail was meticulously considered. It was this attentiveness to detail that gave Mr. Grant Money a decisive competitive edge in his field.

Within the luxurious confines of the Raffles Singapore hotel, a special delivery from the states awaited him. As he unwrapped the package, he discovered not only important documents but also a stack of handwritten thank-you cards. Among them was a heartfelt message from a tribal government leader based in Oklahoma, a recent attendee of Mr. Grant Money's Grant Mastery Academy training.

The tribal leader's gratitude flowed through the words, expressing deep appreciation for the invaluable training they received. The $782,000 grant they had secured was set to transform their community, particularly in the critical phases of community and youth development. They candidly shared that prior attempts had been plagued by common mistakes, only rectified after gaining insights from Mr. Grant Money's training. It was a powerful testament to the impact of education and mentorship.

The letter concluded with an open-hearted invitation, extending a warm welcome for Mr. Grant Money to visit their community whenever he found himself in the area. The sincerity of the message resonated with Mr. Grant Money, affirming that his efforts were indeed making a meaningful difference in the lives of those he touched.

Reflecting on this heartwarming gesture, Mr. Grant Money recognized the exemplary steps taken by the tribal government that led to their success. They had:

1. **Recognized Past Mistakes**: The tribal government acknowledged their previous missteps, demonstrating a willingness to learn and grow.
2. **Invested in Training and Education**: Attending the Grant Mastery Academy training was a pivotal decision, showcasing a commitment to professional development.
3. **Implemented Strategic Changes**: Armed with newfound knowledge, they made purposeful adjustments to their approach, avoiding past pitfalls.
4. **Expressed Gratitude and Fostered Relationships**: The genuine thank-you card and open invitation highlighted the importance of gratitude and building meaningful connections in grant acquisition.

As Mr. Grant Money sat by the pool, overlooking the Singapore skyline, he couldn't help but feel a sense of pride. He was not just securing grants; he was empowering communities to thrive. This encounter served as a powerful reminder that with the right guidance and a willingness to learn, organizations could turn their grant acquisition efforts around, paving the way for a brighter future.

"In the world of grants, meticulous attention to detail is not just a choice, it's a competitive edge that sets you apart from the rest."

- Mr. Grant Money

Exercise: "Turning Mistakes into Success"

This exercise is inspired by the tribal government leader's transformation from grant application mistakes to successful grant acquisition. It encourages self-reflection, learning from past errors, and implementing strategic changes in your grant-seeking or professional endeavors.

Objective: To identify past mistakes, invest in training and education, and implement strategic changes that lead to success in your grant acquisition efforts or professional projects.

Steps:

1. Self-Reflection on Past Mistakes:
- Take a moment to reflect on your past grant applications or professional projects.
- Identify specific mistakes or challenges you encountered that hindered your success.
- Write down these past mistakes to acknowledge them and create a foundation for learning.

2. Identify Areas of Improvement:
- For each mistake identified, analyze which areas of your approach or strategy need improvement.
- Be honest with yourself about where you or your organization fell short.

3. Invest in Training and Education:
- Research training programs, workshops, or educational resources related to grant acquisition or your area of professional interest.
- Choose a program that aligns with your identified areas of improvement.
- Enroll in the selected program and dedicate yourself to learning.

4. Engage in the Learning Process:
- Actively participate in the training program.
- Take notes, ask questions, and seek clarification on topics that were previously challenging for you.
- Utilize the knowledge and insights gained during the training.

5. Develop a Corrective Strategy:
- Based on your training and education, develop a strategy to address the past mistakes you identified.
- Create a step-by-step plan to correct those mistakes and improve your approach.

6. Implement Strategic Changes:
- Begin implementing the corrective strategy in your grant applications or professional projects.
- Be consistent in your efforts to ensure the changes take root.

7. Express Gratitude and Foster Relationships:
- As you make progress and achieve success, express gratitude to those who supported your learning journey.
- Consider writing thank-you cards or letters, acknowledging those who contributed to your development.
- Cultivate positive relationships with mentors, colleagues, or trainers who have been instrumental in your growth.

8. Celebrate Your Achievements:
- Recognize and celebrate your successes, both small and significant.
- Use these achievements as motivation to continue your journey of learning and improvement.

By engaging in this exercise, you'll be able to leverage past mistakes as opportunities for growth and transformation. Learning from errors, investing in education, and implementing strategic changes are key steps in your path to success, whether it's in grant acquisition or any professional endeavor.

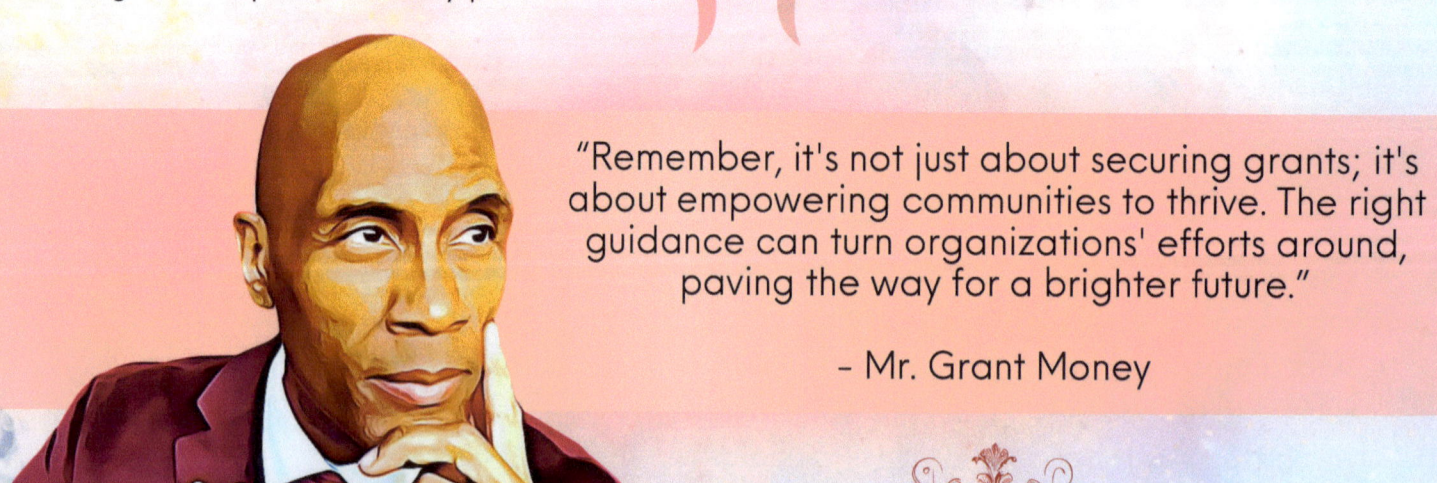

"Remember, it's not just about securing grants; it's about empowering communities to thrive. The right guidance can turn organizations' efforts around, paving the way for a brighter future."

– Mr. Grant Money

Discussion Questions

1. The story highlights the impact of education and mentorship on a tribal government leader's ability to secure a $782,000 grant. How can training programs and mentorship opportunities like the Grant Mastery Academy contribute to the success of nonprofit organizations and government entities in their grant-seeking efforts? What are the key lessons individuals can learn from such programs?

2. The tribal government leader's letter expresses deep gratitude and extends an open invitation to Mr. Grant Money. How important is fostering relationships and expressing gratitude in the world of grant acquisition and nonprofit work? What strategies can organizations employ to build strong and lasting relationships with funders, mentors, and collaborators?

3. The story outlines four steps taken by the tribal government that led to their success. How can organizations and grant seekers recognize their past mistakes, invest in training and education, implement strategic changes, and express gratitude in their grant acquisition endeavors? Can you provide examples of how these steps have been applied successfully by organizations?

4. Mr. Grant Money's attire in the story is described as meticulously detailed, emphasizing the importance of attention to detail in his work. How can meticulous attention to detail play a crucial role in grant proposal writing, grant management, and the overall success of nonprofit organizations? What specific details should grant seekers focus on to enhance their grant applications?

5. The story highlights Mr. Grant Money's sense of pride in empowering communities to thrive. How can the grant acquisition process be seen as a means to create positive and lasting change in communities? What are the long-term effects of successful grant acquisition efforts on the organizations, communities, and individuals they serve?

 Big Idea "Gratitude and Impact Networking Events"

Organize regional or international networking events designed to bring together grant recipients and mentors like Mr. Grant Money. These events would serve as a platform for grant beneficiaries to express their gratitude and share the impact of received grants. It's an opportunity to foster relationships, inspire others, and create a sense of community among organizations striving to make a difference.

🔍 Word Search

Join Mr. Grant Money in the vibrant city of Singapore as he receives a heartfelt message from a tribal leader in Oklahoma, recognizing the impact of his Grant Mastery Academy training. Explore the hidden words within the story that reflect learning, gratitude, change, and the power of mentorship.

In this puzzle, discover the words related to the extraordinary adventures of Mr. Grant Money. Can you find all the hidden words that capture the essence of this remarkable story?

Now, here are the 15 words for the word search puzzle based on the story:

```
P I H S R O T N E M G M T O
N V T N E M T S U J D A R S
S U O L U C I T E M E T A S
I M P A C T L I P E E R N T
E P I R T S N I P A G A S S
M V U T E A U I R O T I F E
P T L V P R E C G R T N O D
O E E I O T I R C M E I R U
W N A T C R R M N E M N M T
E N V E L O P E P N S G A I
R I E R I T T A N L T S T T
A N S I N G A P O R E C I A
O U C O M M U N I T Y R O R
L I N V E S T M E N T T N G
```

ENVELOPE
IMPACT
SINGAPORE
ATTIRE
METICULOUS
SUCCESS
ADJUSTMENT
TRANSFORMATION
EMPOWER
MENTORSHIP
INVESTMENT
COMMUNITY
GRATITUDE
TRAINING
PINSTRIPE

"The heartfelt gesture of gratitude from the tribal government leader highlights the transformative power of education and mentorship. It's a reminder that learning from past mistakes and fostering relationships are crucial elements in the journey to success."

The White Suit of Wisdom: Mr. Grant Money at the Crystal Waters Championship

Empowering Dreams and Lessons in Grant Acquisition

As the extended limousine glided through the bustling streets of Crystal Haven, Mr. Grant Money was a vision of elegant grandeur. His attire was nothing short of spectacular, beginning with an all-white ensemble that exuded timeless sophistication. His wool blue hat, adorned with a simple yet striking band, perfectly complemented his tailored white suit.

Beneath the suit, a pristine white shirt and silk tie added depth to the ensemble. The final touches were his immaculate white Italian leather shoes and an array of accessories, including cufflinks, rings, and a wristwatch that gleamed with understated luxury.

Within the limousine, the low, melodious strains of Miles Davis' "Flamenco Sketches" filled the air, setting a tone of anticipation for the upcoming event. Mr. Grant Money's destination was the prestigious Crystal Waters Championship, but this was no ordinary attendance. He was there to support and witness the achievements of a young man he had personally mentored and nurtured in the arts of grant acquisition and philanthropy – swimmer extraordinaire, Jake Turner.

The events of this year's Crystal Waters Championship were closed to the general public and even families due to COVID restrictions. Still, Mr. Grant Money's presence was a testament to the influential network he had cultivated over the years. His many contacts in high places, grateful for his invaluable assistance in securing grants, opened doors with pleasure whenever he had a need.

As Mr. Grant Money entered the Aqua Dome, his striking all-white attire drew the eyes of those present in the mostly empty, newly built $437 million venue. The hushed murmurs of attendees, hidden behind masks but no less intrigued, revolved around the dashing figure who had graced the event. He moved with the confidence and grace of a distinguished guest of honor, creating an aura of enchantment against the backdrop of the crystal-clear waters and the venue's vibrant blue accents.

Amidst the races and anticipation, Jake Turner's performance was closely watched. The young swimmer had put his heart and soul into this moment, and while he secured a Bronze Medal rather than the gold he had dreamed of, his determination and effort were undeniably commendable. As they embraced after the race, Mr. Grant Money's pride for his protégé was evident. He reminded Jake that sometimes, like in the world of grants, the greatest value comes not from immediate success but from the lessons learned along the way.

With a sage nod, Mr. Grant Money offered words of wisdom that would resonate with Jake and anyone striving for greatness: "Just like with grants, you don't always win or get what you want on the first attempt. What matters is that you extract the valuable lessons from each experience and store them away in your 'Gold Mine' of knowledge." The two smiled, knowing that the Crystal Champions Invitational was just around the corner.

Later that evening, Mr. Grant Money met with dignitaries and contacts before embarking on his journey back to the United States. As he reclined in the comfortable luxury of his private jet, he couldn't help but wonder what new adventures awaited him on his mission to empower nonprofits, government agencies, and individuals to secure the funding they needed to make a difference in the world. With every challenge and triumph, Mr. Grant Money continued to redefine the art of grant acquisition and philanthropy, leaving a legacy that would inspire generations to come.

> "Just like with grants, you don't always win or get what you want on the first attempt. What matters is that you extract the valuable lessons from each experience and store them away in your 'Gold Mine' of knowledge."
> - Mr. Grant Money

Exercise: "The Gold Mine Reflection Journey"

Objective: To foster resilience, self-reflection, and personal growth by drawing parallels between life experiences, setbacks, and the pursuit of success in different realms.

Materials Needed:
- Paper pen a quiet space for contemplation.

Steps:

1. Create Your Vision Board (15 minutes):
- Begin by creating a vision board that represents your personal and professional goals. Use magazines, images, or drawings to visualize your aspirations.

2. Identify Your "Gold Mine" (10 minutes):
- Reflect on your past experiences, both successes, and setbacks. Identify the lessons you've learned from each, considering the wisdom gained from challenges.

3. Analyze Your Grant Applications (20 minutes):
- Metaphorically view your life as a series of grant applications. Consider instances where you faced obstacles or didn't achieve immediate success. Identify the valuable lessons embedded in those experiences.

4. Dress for Success (15 minutes):
- Select an outfit that makes you feel confident and powerful. Wear it and notice how your posture and mindset shift. Consider how appearance influences confidence and success, as observed in Mr. Grant Money's attire.

5. Soundtrack of Your Life (10 minutes):
- Create a playlist that reflects different phases of your life journey. Choose songs that resonate with moments of triumph, resilience, and personal growth. As you listen, reflect on the parallels with Mr. Grant Money's musical accompaniment.

6. Dine with Your Mentors (30 minutes):
- Imagine having dinner with mentors, real or fictional, who have guided you through challenges. Write down the advice they would offer based on Mr. Grant Money's mentorship to Jake Turner.

Discussion Questions

1. What role does Mr. Grant Money's extravagant attire and presence play in shaping the atmosphere and perception of the Crystal Waters Championship, and how does it reflect on his character and influence in the philanthropic world?

2. The story emphasizes the significance of learning from experiences, both in the world of grants and swimming. How do you interpret Mr. Grant Money's advice about creating a 'Gold Mine' of knowledge, and how might this perspective apply to individuals pursuing success in different fields?

3. In the context of the COVID restrictions and closed-door events, how does Mr. Grant Money's ability to secure access to the Crystal Waters Championship illustrate the power of networking and connections in the realm of philanthropy?

4. Jake Turner's Bronze Medal victory is portrayed as a commendable achievement despite falling short of his gold-medal aspirations. In what ways can this narrative be applied to the broader theme of resilience and perseverance in the pursuit of goals, whether in sports, philanthropy, or other endeavors?

5. Mr. Grant Money's journey to empower nonprofits, government agencies, and individuals is highlighted as a continuous mission filled with challenges and triumphs. How might his story inspire others to rethink their approach to philanthropy and grant acquisition, and what lessons can be drawn from his legacy for those aspiring to make a positive impact in the world?

 Big Idea "Funding Lessons in Unconventional Settings"

Develop a series of educational events and seminars that take place in unique and unconventional settings. These events could be designed to teach grant acquisition skills and philanthropy lessons while inspiring participants with creativity and out-of-the-box thinking. Much like Mr. Grant Money's appearance at the Paralympics, such events can make learning an unforgettable experience.

🔍 Word Search

Welcome to the "Mr. Grant Money Wordsearch Puzzle," a tribute to the man who embodies elegance, sophistication, and the art of philanthropy. Immerse yourself in the world of Mr. Grant Money as he graces the Crystal Waters Championship with his presence, mentoring the next generation of philanthropic leaders. Discover the words that encapsulate his journey and the invaluable lessons he imparts along the way.

In this puzzle, discover the words related to the extraordinary adventures of Mr. Grant Money. Can you find all the hidden words that capture the essence of this remarkable story?

Now, here are the 14 words for the word search puzzle based on the story:

I	N	P	T	N	N	P	T	T	L	I	A	A	P
U	Y	H	R	N	R	M	J	O	U	R	N	E	Y
E	Y	I	I	L	E	U	P	R	E	G	O	L	D
S	T	L	U	D	E	Y	E	N	O	M	P	N	L
W	H	A	M	I	E	G	E	L	E	G	A	N	T
I	L	N	P	G	E	M	A	R	O	T	N	E	M
M	I	T	H	N	M	T	I	C	H	I	D	L	M
M	M	H	N	I	O	T	P	D	Y	O	E	A	T
E	O	R	E	T	D	G	Q	N	I	Y	T	U	T
R	U	O	P	A	E	I	E	E	G	P	S	Q	R
A	S	P	M	R	A	N	D	H	G	E	U	A	I
E	I	Y	U	I	T	N	A	R	G	I	A	M	R
U	N	O	Y	E	O	E	I	U	L	R	C	T	P
L	E	T	H	S	A	E	N	P	U	O	I	H	E

SWIMMER
DOME
DIGNITARIES
TRIUMPH
AQUA
GOLD
GRANT
JOURNEY
LEGACY
MONEY
MENTOR
PHILANTHROPY
ELEGANT
LIMOUSINE

"Crystal Waters Championship are a testament to the power of mentorship and support. This journey reflects the perseverance and commitment to excellence that can inspire generations."
- Mr. Grant Money

Unlocking the Seven Keys to Grant Success in a Changing World

Mr. Grant Money's Harvard Lecture: Navigating the Post-COVID Grant Landscape

The phone call from the ecstatic city manager in the upper regions of Wisconsin came like a whirlwind of excitement. He was speaking so rapidly that Mr. Grant Money had trouble keeping up with his words. Amid the frenzied chatter, the city manager managed to convey the incredible news – their city had just secured its largest grant in history, and much of the credit was owed to Mr. Grant Money's guidance and direction.

In his characteristically calm and self-assured style, Mr. Grant Money responded, assuring the city manager that this was just the beginning. He encouraged them to stay the course, for even greater achievements lay ahead.

Word of Mr. Grant Money's exceptional victories and accomplishments in helping cities, states, tribal governments, and nonprofits secure funding reached the ears of the prestigious Harvard University John F. Kennedy School of Government. They extended an invitation for him to speak at a special symposium, where he would be the featured guest.

Mr. Grant Money accepted the invitation on one condition – that the university would charter a top-of-the-line bus to bring a classroom of underserved 9th graders and provide them with front-row seats at the event. He believed in inspiring the next generation to dream big and achieve more, and this was his opportunity to do just that. Harvard University readily agreed.

The day of the symposium arrived, and the lecture hall was filled to capacity. As promised, the ninth graders were bused in and treated like royalty. For most of them, it was their first time setting foot on a college or university campus. Mr. Grant Money personally greeted each student, taking photos and signing autographs in his latest book, which featured his inspiring slogan, "Be Brave... Be Bold... and Be Brilliant!"

Among the students, Patrick Jones, a quiet and reserved young man, secretly shed a tear. He confided in one of the chaperones that he had often felt forgotten and overlooked. This event, and Mr. Grant Money's presence, had proven to him and his classmates that they were not forgotten and that opportunities beyond their wildest dreams were within reach.

After learning about what Patrick conveyed to the chaperone, Mr. Grant Money reached into his stylish leather briefcase and gave Patrick one of his favorite books, written by a man who went to Harvard, Reginald Lewis. Patrick looked at the book and read the title, which said, "Why Should White Guys Have All the Fun?"

Mr. Grant Money told him there's a building on this campus named after him, the Reginald F. Lewis Law Center, and that Patrick could achieve greatness too, just like Reginald did. Patrick's eyes lit up with newfound hope and determination as he held the book in his hands, realizing that his dreams were indeed attainable.

Mr. Grant Money, true to form, appeared on stage dressed impeccably in a regal outfit that radiated polished elegance. His attire was a symphony of sophistication, from his tailored suit to his choice of accessories. He began his lecture, captivating the audience for 35-minutes as he shared the challenges, progress, and current state of the grant and philanthropic landscape.

Students and professors alike posed thoughtful questions, and Mr. Grant Money answered each one with the wisdom of a Grant Wizard. A student from India, speaking in a dialect that initially posed a challenge for comprehension, asked a profound question: "In the changing post-COVID world, what must cities and states do to secure the most grant money?"

Mr. Grant Money, with his signature eloquence, responded by listing seven keys to success in the evolving grant landscape. His insights left the audience in awe, and the young student from India nodded in appreciation.

As Mr. Grant Money concluded his lecture, he couldn't help but reflect on the importance of ensuring that the 9th graders were invited to experience this transformative event. It reminded him of the support and encouragement he had received from individuals like Bob Ray Sanders and the Dallas-Fort Worth Association of Black Journalists when he was their age. With that in mind, he left the symposium knowing that he had sown the seeds of inspiration in the hearts and minds of those who would shape the future.

Here are seven keys to success in the evolving grant landscape as shared by Mr. Grant Money during his lecture:

1. **Adaptability and Resilience**: Organizations must be adaptable to changing circumstances, especially in a post-COVID world. Resilience is key to weathering unforeseen challenges.
2. **Strategic Collaboration**: Building strong partnerships and collaborations with other organizations, both within and outside your sector, can lead to more substantial grant opportunities.
3. **Data-Driven Decision-Making**: Utilize data and analytics to support your grant applications. Show funders the measurable impact of your programs and initiatives.
4. **Innovation and Creativity**: Grant funders are often looking for fresh and innovative approaches to address pressing issues. Don't be afraid to think outside the box.
5. **Diversity, Equity, and Inclusion**: Embrace diversity and inclusivity in your organization's leadership and programs. Many funders prioritize projects that promote social equity and inclusion.
6. **Clear and Compelling Storytelling**: Craft compelling narratives that resonate with funders. Your story should clearly communicate the problem you're addressing, your solution, and the impact you aim to achieve.
7. **Long-Term Sustainability**: Show funders how your organization plans to sustain its programs beyond the grant period. Demonstrating financial stability and a plan for continued impact is crucial.

These seven keys reflect the evolving priorities of grant funders and provide organizations with a roadmap to success in securing grant funding in today's dynamic landscape.

Exercise: "Mapping Your Journey to Grant Success in a Changing World"

This exercise encourages individuals, organizations, and grant seekers to apply Mr. Grant Money's seven keys to success in the evolving grant landscape to their own grant acquisition strategies.

Objective: To reflect on your grant-seeking efforts and map out strategies that align with the seven keys shared by Mr. Grant Money.

Steps:

1. Self-Assessment:
- Take a moment to reflect on your recent grant-seeking experiences or your organization's grant efforts. Identify areas where you've succeeded and challenges you've faced.

2. Seven Key Analysis:
- Consider each of the seven keys to success shared by Mr. Grant Money:
  - Adaptability and Resilience
  - Strategic Collaboration
  - Data-Driven Decision-Making
  - Innovation and Creativity
  - Diversity, Equity, and Inclusion
  - Clear and Compelling Storytelling
  - Long-Term Sustainability

3. Key Alignment:
- For each key, assess how well your recent grant-seeking efforts align with it. Are there areas where your approach reflects the key's principles, or are there areas for improvement?

4. Strengths and Weaknesses:
- Identify the strengths in your grant-seeking strategy that align with the keys. Also, acknowledge areas where your approach could be strengthened or adapted to better meet these principles.

5. Actionable Plan:
- Develop a plan that outlines specific actions you or your organization will take to improve alignment with the seven keys. Be as specific as possible, listing steps, responsibilities, and timelines.

6. Measurable Goals:
- Set measurable goals for each key. What outcomes or achievements would signify success for each key? For example, you might set a goal to establish two new strategic collaborations within the next year.

7. Regular Evaluation:
- Commit to regular evaluations of your progress. Schedule check-in points to review your alignment with the seven keys and make necessary adjustments to your strategy.

8. Celebrate Successes:
- Celebrate your successes as you make progress toward achieving your goals. Recognize and appreciate your efforts and adaptability.

By mapping your grant-seeking journey to these seven keys and setting clear goals for alignment, you'll be better equipped to navigate the changing grant landscape, secure funding, and make a more significant impact in the evolving post-COVID world.

> "In this ever-changing world, adaptability and resilience are your armor, and strategic collaboration is your sword in the battle for grant success."
> - Mr. Grant Money

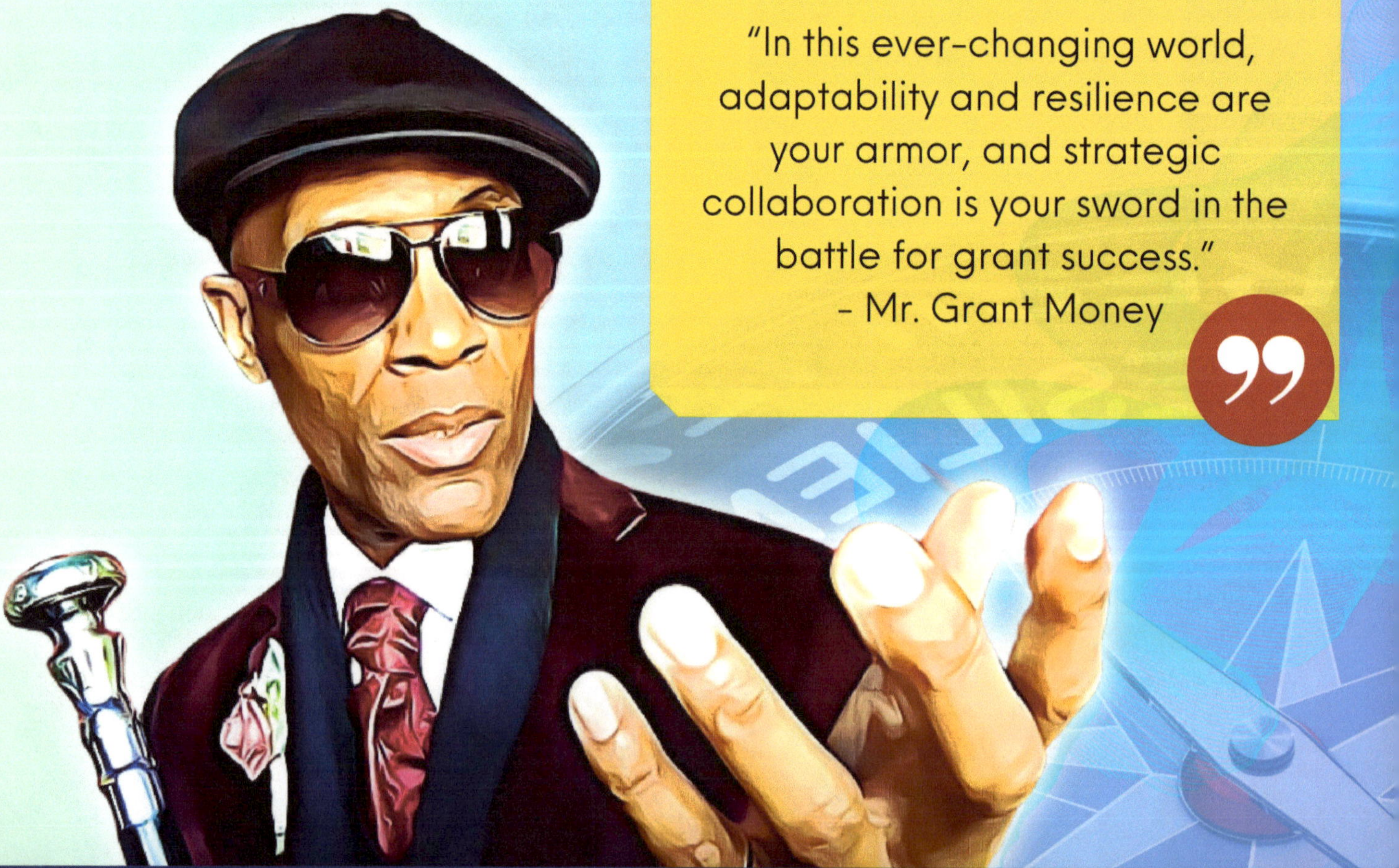

Discussion Questions

1. The story emphasizes Mr. Grant Money's commitment to inspiring the next generation by bringing underserved 9th graders to Harvard for his lecture. How can educational institutions and successful individuals play a role in inspiring and mentoring underserved youth to pursue their dreams and opportunities? What impact can such initiatives have on young people's aspirations and future success?

2. Mr. Grant Money shared seven keys to success in the evolving grant landscape during his lecture. How do these keys, such as adaptability, data-driven decision-making, and diversity, apply to organizations seeking grant funding in a post-COVID world? What are some practical steps organizations can take to implement these keys in their grant-seeking strategies?

3. The story highlights Patrick Jones, a young student who found inspiration and determination from Mr. Grant Money's lecture and the gift of a book by Reginald Lewis. How can a single moment of inspiration or mentorship impact a young person's life and future choices? What role can mentors and role models play in nurturing the potential of underserved youth?

4. The seven keys to success in the evolving grant landscape reflect shifting priorities among grant funders. What are some emerging trends or priorities in the world of grants and philanthropy, especially in light of the challenges posed by the COVID-19 pandemic? How can organizations stay aligned with these evolving priorities and enhance their grant-seeking strategies?

5. Mr. Grant Money's commitment to fostering adaptability, collaboration, and innovation in organizations seeking grant funding is evident in the keys to success he shared during his lecture. How can organizations create a culture that embraces these principles and fosters continuous improvement in their grant acquisition efforts? What are some practical ways to promote adaptability and innovation in a grant-seeking organization?

 Big Idea "Student Outreach Scholarships"

Encourage educational institutions, particularly universities and colleges, to create programs that connect underprivileged high school students with inspirational events like symposiums or guest lectures. These scholarships could cover the cost of attending such events, offering young minds the chance to be inspired and exposed to a broader world of possibilities.

🔍 Word Search

Dive into the world of Mr. Grant Money, where elegance, mentorship, and philanthropy converge. Explore the story of an extraordinary day at Harvard University's John F. Kennedy School of Government, where Mr. Grant Money imparted his wisdom and left an indelible mark on both students and scholars.

In this puzzle, discover the words related to the extraordinary adventures of Mr. Grant Money. Can you find all the hidden words that capture the essence of this remarkable story?

Now, here are the 14 words for the word search puzzle based on the story:

H	A	R	V	A	R	D	C	O	O	I	A	I	I
L	N	T	M	E	N	T	O	R	S	H	I	P	M
Y	I	O	V	P	A	D	I	D	I	E	T	S	P
T	S	T	O	R	Y	T	E	L	L	I	N	G	A
I	Y	N	P	L	A	R	M	S	I	I	O	O	C
S	Y	P	O	R	H	T	N	A	L	I	H	P	T
R	F	E	P	H	I	L	O	S	O	P	H	E	R
E	R	E	S	I	L	I	E	N	C	E	R	N	E
V	N	O	I	T	A	R	O	B	A	L	L	O	C
I	T	I	N	S	P	I	R	A	T	I	O	N	N
D	H	I	N	N	O	V	A	T	I	O	N	R	M
N	O	I	T	A	N	I	M	R	E	T	E	D	P
R	A	A	P	L	I	N	C	L	U	S	I	O	N
T	R	A	N	S	F	O	R	M	A	T	I	O	N

IMPACT
PHILANTHROPY
INCLUSION
DIVERSITY
INSPIRATION
COLLABORATION
INNOVATION
TRANSFORMATION
DETERMINATION
PHILOSOPHER
HARVARD
STORYTELLING
RESILIENCE
MENTORSHIP

"Inspiring the next generation isn't just about opening doors; it's about handing them the keys to unlock their potential."

Secrets of the Grant Whisperer: Mr. Grant Money's Monte Carlo Coup

Navigating High-Stakes Galas and Securing Multi-Million-Dollar Grants

In the dimly lit hallways of a prestigious charity gala in Monte Carlo, Mr. Grant Money moved with the grace of a panther, his eyes hidden behind his signature shades as he navigated the sea of tuxedos and gowns. He had been called upon for a mission of utmost importance: securing a multi-million-dollar grant for a top-secret environmental project that would change the course of history.

As he mingled with the world's elite, Mr. Grant Money used his charm and charisma to gather critical information. His keen ears picked up whispers of rival organizations vying for the same grant, and his mind calculated strategies to outmaneuver them.

With a glass of vintage champagne in one hand and his Gold-Mine Journal in the other, Mr. Grant Money moved stealthily towards the heart of the gala—the billionaire philanthropist known as "The Jaguar." The Jaguar was known for his elusive nature and his passion for saving endangered species.

Engaging The Jaguar in conversation, Mr. Grant Money artfully steered their discussion toward the environmental project, subtly dropping hints about the urgency of the situation. He recounted stories of how he had helped organizations in similar dire straits secure vital funding, all while maintaining his mystique as a Master Grant Acquisition Specialist.

The Jaguar's interest was piqued, and he leaned in to listen intently. Mr. Grant Money seized the moment and presented a concise yet compelling case for why this project deserved his support. He shared statistics, success stories, and a compelling vision for the future—a world where endangered species thrived and ecosystems were restored.

The room seemed to fade away as The Jaguar considered Mr. Grant Money's words. He nodded in agreement, and the deal was sealed. A multi-million-dollar grant was pledged to the environmental project, a victory for nature and conservation.

As Mr. Grant Money exited the gala, he reflected on the lessons learned from this mission. He knew that in the world of grant acquisition, preparation, persistence, and the ability to connect with potential donors were paramount. He scribbled in his Gold-Mine Journal, "Lesson: **Building genuine connections and effectively communicating your vision can turn a chance encounter into a life-changing grant**."

With a satisfied smile and the knowledge that he had once again made a profound impact, Mr. Grant Money vanished into the night, ready for his next adventure in the world of grant acquisition.

Exercise: "The Power of Persuasive Storytelling in Grant Acquisition"

This exercise focuses on enhancing your ability to use persuasive storytelling when seeking grants. Mr. Grant Money's success in securing a multi-million-dollar grant hinged on his effective storytelling during the gala. Use this exercise to hone your storytelling skills.

Objective: To develop your skills in persuasive storytelling for grant acquisition.

Steps:

1. Select Your Project:
- Choose a specific project or cause for which you're seeking grant funding. It could be a nonprofit initiative, community project, or any idea you're passionate about.

2. Identify Your Target Audience:
- Determine the primary individuals or organizations you need to engage with to secure the grant. Identify their interests, values, and motivations.

3. Develop Your Story:
- Craft a compelling and concise narrative about your project or initiative. Your story should be structured to highlight the urgency and impact of your cause. Consider these elements:
  - Introduction: Start with a captivating hook that draws your audience in.
  - Problem Statement: Describe the issue or challenge your project aims to address.
  - Impact: Explain the positive outcomes your project will achieve, focusing on the change it will bring.
  - Personal Connection: Share anecdotes or stories that illustrate the human element and the difference your project will make.
  - Call to Action: Clearly state what you're requesting and why it's essential for the audience.

4. Gather Data and Facts:
- Collect relevant data, statistics, and examples that support your story. Use this information to substantiate the urgency and importance of your project.

5. Practice Your Delivery:
- Rehearse delivering your story in a persuasive and engaging manner. Focus on clarity, enthusiasm, and emotion. Practice with friends or colleagues for feedback.

6. Feedback and Refinement:
- Share your story with a trusted group and gather feedback. Ask for suggestions on how to make your storytelling more compelling and persuasive.

7. Engage Your Target Audience:
- Contact your target audience and use your persuasive storytelling to convey your project's significance and impact. This could be in meetings, presentations, emails, or grant applications.

8. Follow Up:
- Continue engaging with your target audience, answer any questions they may have, and reiterate the importance of your project.

9. Track Your Progress:
- Keep records of your interactions, responses, and outcomes. This will help you refine your storytelling in the future.

10. Celebrate Your Successes:
- If you secure the grant or receive positive feedback, celebrate your storytelling achievement and recognize the impact of your effective communication.

Effective persuasive storytelling is a valuable skill in the world of grant acquisition. By refining your narrative and using it to convey the urgency and importance of your projects, you can increase your chances of securing grants and making a meaningful difference in your community or field.

Discussion Questions

1. In this thrilling story, Mr. Grant Money demonstrates the art of securing multi-million-dollar grants through charm, charisma, and effective communication. How important are interpersonal skills and the ability to build genuine connections in the world of grant acquisition? Can you share an example of a situation where strong interpersonal skills made a significant difference in securing funding or partnerships?

2. The story emphasizes the importance of preparation and persistence in grant acquisition. What are some key steps organizations and individuals should take when preparing to secure a substantial grant, especially for high-stakes projects? How can persistence be balanced with adaptability in the face of challenges?

3. Mr. Grant Money's ability to effectively communicate a compelling vision played a central role in securing the multi-million-dollar grant. How important is storytelling in grant acquisition, and how can organizations and individuals craft narratives that resonate with potential donors or grant-making organizations? Can you think of an example where a well-told story significantly impacted the success of a grant application?

4. The story features "The Jaguar," a billionaire philanthropist with a passion for conservation. How can organizations identify and approach potential donors or philanthropists who align with their mission and projects? What are some strategies for engaging philanthropists or donors effectively and compelling them to support a cause?

5. Mr. Grant Money's approach in the gala involves subtlety and strategic communication. What are some ethical considerations when pursuing grant opportunities or philanthropic donations, especially in competitive situations? How can individuals and organizations maintain integrity and transparency in their grant acquisition efforts?

💡 Big Idea "The Grant Acquisition Mixer"

Create a unique networking event that combines the elements of a charity gala and a business mixer. The event should bring together grant seekers, grant providers, and experts in an elegant yet relaxed atmosphere. This setting allows for genuine connections, fostering relationships that could lead to successful grant applications. To add an extra layer of charm, the event could be held in a prestigious or exotic location to capture the essence of Mr. Grant Money's adventures.

🔍 Word Search

Embark on a journey to the prestigious charity gala in Monte Carlo with Mr. Grant Money, the Master Grant Acquisition Specialist. In this word search puzzle, you'll explore the art of securing grants amidst a sea of tuxedos and gowns.

In this puzzle, discover the words related to the extraordinary adventures of Mr. Grant Money. Can you find all the hidden words that capture the essence of this remarkable story?

Now, here are the 13 words for the word search puzzle based on the story:

R	S	N	O	I	T	A	Z	I	N	A	G	R	O
S	E	I	Y	G	E	T	A	R	T	S	S	T	A
R	P	N	P	E	R	S	I	S	T	E	N	C	E
P	R	E	R	R	R	E	T	N	U	O	C	N	E
G	E	A	C	T	O	S	N	Y	I	O	E	G	E
A	C	T	N	I	C	J	T	S	G	G	A	E	Y
A	G	S	I	T	A	I	E	E	R	L	A	N	O
R	R	A	J	O	R	L	L	C	A	E	N	O	E
O	E	E	E	A	N	C	I	A	T	N	O	D	O
C	I	O	H	G	A	T	R	S	V	N	C	O	I
S	C	C	O	E	S	N	L	A	T	I	G	N	N
P	R	E	P	A	R	A	T	I	O	N	R	O	N
U	R	G	E	N	C	Y	C	A	U	P	S	R	S
C	O	N	S	E	R	V	A	T	I	O	N	S	T

PROJECT
RIVAL
URGENCY
GALA
ORGANIZATIONS
CONSERVATION
CHARITY
SPECIALIST
PERSISTENCE
DONORS
PREPARATION
STRATEGY
ENCOUNTER

"Great achievements are born from the fusion of passion and purpose. When two minds connect with a shared vision, the world can change."

Winning the Grantopoly Game: Mr. Grant Money's San Diego Saga

From Challenges to Triumphs - The Blueprint for Grant Acquisition Dominance

In the sun-soaked city of San Diego, a new era in grant acquisition was about to dawn, and it was all thanks to the enigmatic and stylish Mr. Grant Money. The story of this adventure would soon be dubbed "Grantopoly," an homage to the monopoly the San Diego School District was destined to have over the world of grant funding.

It all began when Dr. Isabella Ramirez, the School District Superintendent, reached out to Mr. Grant Money in a state of desperation. The district's schools were struggling, and their dreams of innovative programs and state-of-the-art facilities seemed to be slipping through their fingers.

Mr. Grant Money, dressed impeccably in a navy pinstripe suit and a striking red tie, met with Dr. Ramirez and her team in a secluded, upscale cafe overlooking the Pacific Ocean. As the waves crashed in the background, he listened intently to their challenges and aspirations.

The lesson from his Gold-Mine Journal that day was clear: "Even the greatest challenges can be overcome with the right strategy and unwavering determination."

With that lesson in mind, Mr. Grant Money embarked on a mission to transform the fortunes of the San Diego School District. He knew that to create a Grantopoly, he needed to identify and seize every available grant opportunity, large or small.

Weeks turned into months, and Mr. Grant Money's team meticulously researched, curated, and customized grant proposals for every conceivable grantor. They tailored their pitches to highlight the unique needs and strengths of each school in the district, from underserved communities to elite institutions.

Mr. Grant Money utilized his extensive network to arrange meetings with influential donors, city officials, and philanthropic powerhouses. He knew that building relationships was the cornerstone of grant acquisition success.

The superintendent's office soon became a hub of excitement as news of grant victories poured in. The School District of San Diego was awarded funding for everything from STEM programs to arts initiatives, sports facilities to mental health resources. They even secured grants to improve school infrastructure and create sustainable, energy-efficient campuses.

As the victories continued, the term "Grantopoly" was coined, symbolizing the district's unrivaled success in the world of grant funding. They had a monopoly on winning grants, and it showed in their revitalized schools and thriving student communities.

The valuable lesson that emerged from this epic journey was clear: "Comprehensive research, personalized pitches, strategic networking, and persistence are the keys to creating a Grantopoly in grant acquisition."

As the sun set over the Pacific, Mr. Grant Money knew that the School District of San Diego had embarked on a new chapter of success, and the grant funding victories would keep rolling in. With a final sip of his tea, he made a note in his Gold-Mine Journal, "Grantopoly achieved. Onward to new horizons!"

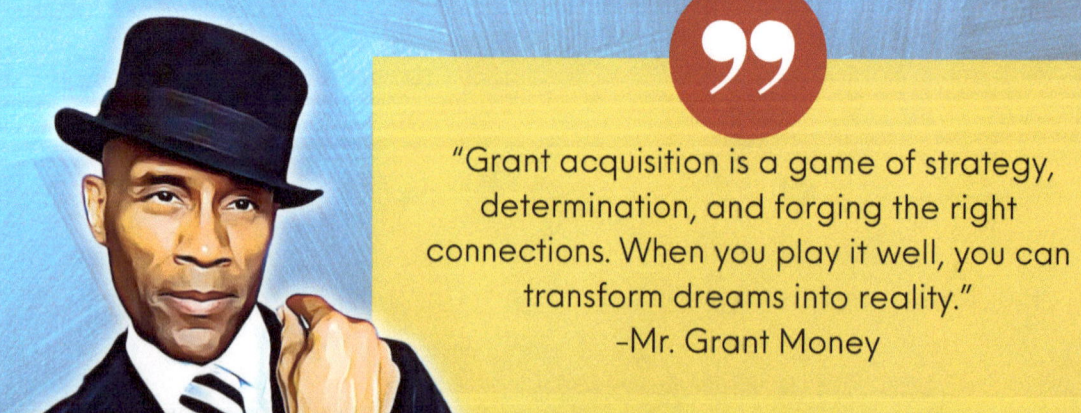

"Grant acquisition is a game of strategy, determination, and forging the right connections. When you play it well, you can transform dreams into reality."
-Mr. Grant Money

Exercise: "Building Your Grant Acquisition Strategy"

This exercise is designed to help you develop a structured grant acquisition strategy inspired by Mr. Grant Money's successful approach in the San Diego saga.

Objective: Create a comprehensive grant acquisition strategy that leverages research, personalization, networking, and persistence.

Steps:

1. Select Your Project or Cause:
- Choose a specific project or cause for which you seek grant funding. It could be related to education, community development, healthcare, the environment, or any area you are passionate about.

2. Research Grants:
- Conduct thorough research to identify potential grant opportunities related to your project or cause. Utilize online databases, foundation websites, government grants, and industry-specific resources. Make a list of relevant grants.

3. Prioritize Grants:
- Evaluate the grants you've identified and prioritize them based on criteria such as alignment with your project, application deadlines, grantor reputation, and potential impact.

4. Customize Your Pitches:
- Create personalized grant proposals for each prioritized grant. Tailor your pitches to address the specific needs and goals of the grantor. Highlight how your project aligns with their mission and objectives.

5. Network and Build Relationships:
- Identify key individuals, organizations, or decision-makers within the grantor's network. Leverage your existing contacts and use professional networking platforms like LinkedIn to connect with them.

6. Arrange Meetings and Engagements:
- Reach out to potential grantors to express your interest in their grant opportunities. Request meetings or informational sessions to discuss your project and explore potential collaborations.

7. Prepare for Effective Presentations:
- If you secure meetings or presentations, be well-prepared to articulate your project's objectives, needs, and potential impact. Craft compelling narratives to convey the importance of your cause.

8. Seek Feedback and Guidance:
- Collaborate with mentors, advisors, or experts in grant acquisition to refine your grant proposals and presentation skills.

9. Submission and Follow-Up:
- Submit your grant applications by their respective deadlines, ensuring all required documents are included. After submission, follow up with grantors to confirm receipt and inquire about the evaluation timeline.

10. Persistence and Adaptation:
- Be persistent in your pursuit of grant funding. If you receive rejections, view them as opportunities for improvement. Adapt your strategy based on feedback and changing circumstances.

11. Evaluate and Learn:
- After each grant application, assess what worked well and what could be improved. Continuously refine your approach based on lessons learned.

12. Celebrate Your Victories:
- When you secure grants, celebrate your achievements, and recognize the impact your successful grant acquisition has on your chosen cause or project.

Building a structured grant acquisition strategy, much like Mr. Grant Money in the San Diego saga, increases your chances of securing funding for your important initiatives. Use this strategy to make a meaningful impact and achieve your grant acquisition goals.

"In the world of grants, every challenge is an opportunity waiting to be seized, and every school, no matter its background, deserves a shot at success."

- Mr. Grant Money

Discussion Questions

1. The story of "Grantopoly" in San Diego highlights the importance of comprehensive research, personalized pitches, strategic networking, and persistence in grant acquisition. How do these key elements apply to grant acquisition efforts in various sectors and organizations? Can you share examples of how one or more of these elements have made a significant difference in securing grants?

2. Mr. Grant Money's extensive network played a crucial role in the success of the San Diego School District. How can organizations and individuals effectively build and leverage networks to enhance their grant acquisition efforts? What are some strategies for establishing and nurturing valuable relationships with potential donors or grantors?

3. The story emphasizes the transformation of the San Diego School District through grant funding. What are some common challenges faced by educational institutions when it comes to securing grants, and how can they overcome these challenges? How do grant opportunities vary for different levels of education, from K-12 to higher education?

4. Mr. Grant Money's Gold-Mine Journal provides valuable lessons for grant acquisition. How important is the documentation of experiences and lessons learned in the process of securing grants? Can you think of instances where keeping a record of past successes and failures has proven beneficial in future grant applications or fundraising efforts?

5. "Grantopoly" symbolizes the unparalleled success of the San Diego School District in grant funding. What can other organizations and communities learn from the district's experience in building a strong grant acquisition strategy and fostering a culture of success? How might the concept of "Grantopoly" apply to other regions or sectors, and what challenges might they face in achieving similar results?

 Big Idea The Grantopoly Challenge for Schools

Organize a friendly competition among schools or school districts to encourage them to improve their grant acquisition strategies. Schools can participate in the "Grantopoly Challenge" by competing to secure grants for specific projects. This initiative not only promotes healthy competition but also fosters a culture of grant acquisition excellence. Schools can share their experiences, lessons, and tips, creating a supportive community of grant seekers striving for success. The most successful participants can be recognized and rewarded for their achievements.

🔍 Word Search

Join Mr. Grant Money in the vibrant city of San Diego as he embarks on a mission to create a "Grantopoly" for the San Diego School District.

In this puzzle, discover the words related to the extraordinary adventures of Mr. Grant Money. Can you find all the hidden words that capture the essence of this remarkable story?

Now, here are the 15 words for the word search puzzle based on the story:

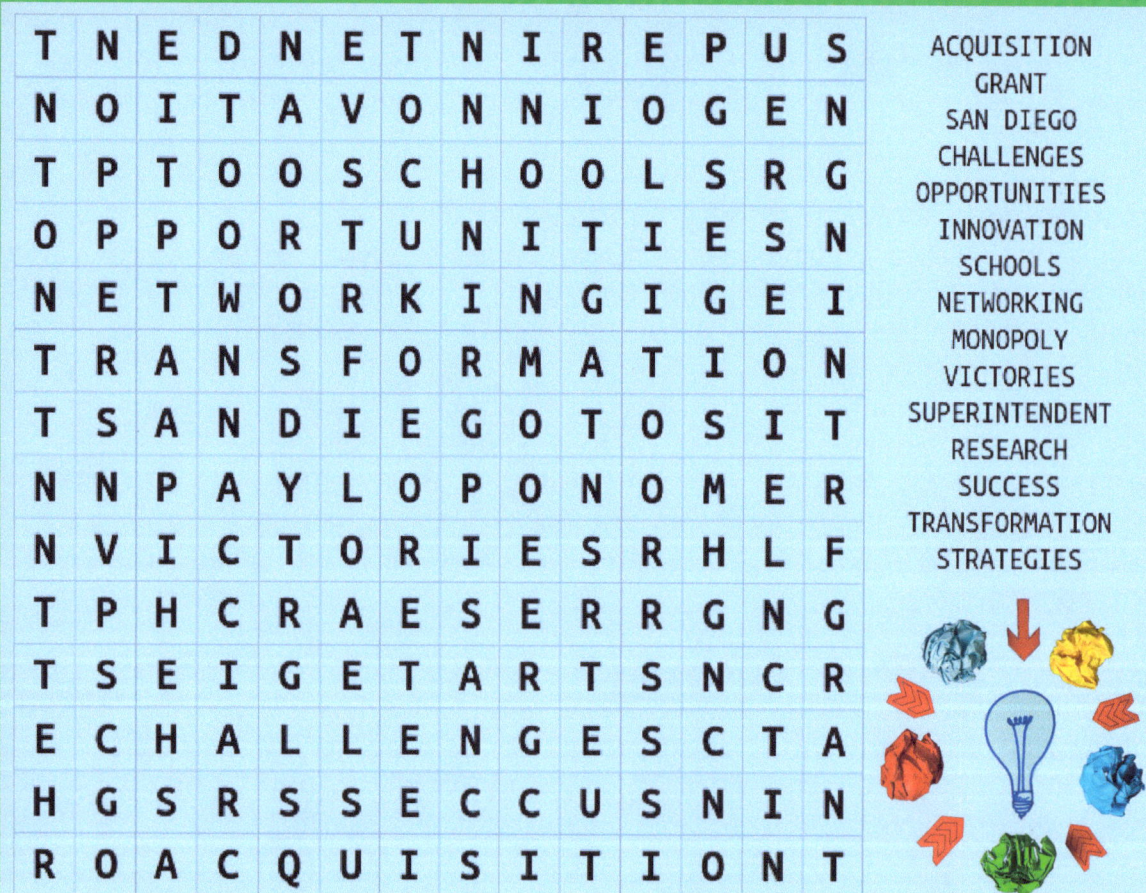

ACQUISITION
GRANT
SAN DIEGO
CHALLENGES
OPPORTUNITIES
INNOVATION
SCHOOLS
NETWORKING
MONOPOLY
VICTORIES
SUPERINTENDENT
RESEARCH
SUCCESS
TRANSFORMATION
STRATEGIES

"Success isn't about the cards you're dealt; it's how well you play your hand. With the right strategy, even the most challenging situations can lead to triumph."

Granting the Impossible: Mr. Grant Money's Celestial Revelation

When Cosmic Visitors Unleash the Power of Grant-Making Brilliance

In the bustling heart of London, Mr. Grant Money found himself aboard a sleek, high-speed train heading to an important meeting with a philanthropic organization. His attire was nothing short of impeccable – a charcoal gray tailored suit, a crisp white shirt, and his signature MGM cufflinks gleaming like polished silver. His hat, shades, and other stylish accessories added an air of sophistication that followed him everywhere he went.

As the train's rhythmic clatter filled the air, Mr. Grant Money, feeling somewhat jet-lagged from his recent globetrotting adventures, leaned back in his plush leather seat. The gentle rocking of the train and the low hum of conversation from other passengers began to lull him into a peaceful slumber.

But then, something extraordinary happened. In the midst of his reverie, Mr. Grant Money was once again visited by the enigmatic extraterrestrial beings that had crossed his path before. They surrounded him in their peculiar way, their movements graceful and ethereal, their language incomprehensible.

This time, their attention was drawn to Mr. Grant Money's scepter – the one that most often was mistaken for a cane. In their delicate touch, they weaved a shimmering energy around it, infusing it with cosmic power.

Mr. Grant Money awoke with a start, the memory of their visit vivid and surreal. He glanced at the scepter, which now seemed to pulsate with an otherworldly energy. Tentatively, he placed a finger atop it, and in an instant, his mind was flooded with a cascade of brilliant ideas and solutions to grant acquisition challenges he had faced in the past. The lesson from this unexpected encounter was abundantly clear:

"Inspiration can strike in the most unexpected of places, and innovation often comes from embracing the unknown."

As Mr. Grant Money jotted down the newfound ideas in his Gold-Mine Journal, he couldn't help but smile. The crying baby in the nearby seat seemed to have quieted, and for a moment, he wondered if the cosmic visitation had all been a dream. But the newfound insights and solutions were all too real, and he knew he had been touched by something extraordinary.

Mr. Grant Money was wise enough to know that most people would not understand that he truly had encounters with alien forces, so he decided to keep his special power and chance encounter with beings of higher intelligence to himself, wrapped in tales, and placed in his treasured journal. These encounters were his secret well of inspiration, a source of innovation that set him apart in the world of grant acquisition.

With newfound inspiration and determination, Mr. Grant Money continued his journey to the philanthropic meeting in London. Little did he know that the profound ideas from the cosmic encounter would soon pave the way for groundbreaking grant acquisitions, leaving a lasting impact on the world of philanthropy.

Exercise: "Harvesting Cosmic Inspiration for Creative Problem-Solving"

This exercise encourages you to explore unconventional sources of inspiration and creativity to overcome challenges, much like Mr. Grant Money's celestial revelation. It will help you tap into your inner innovator and approach problem-solving from a different perspective.

Objective: Unlock your creative potential by seeking inspiration from unexpected and unfamiliar sources.

Steps:

1. Identify a Challenge or Problem:
- Select a specific challenge or problem you're currently facing. It could be related to your work, personal goals, or a creative project.

2. Create a Relaxing Environment:
- Find a quiet and comfortable space where you can relax and let your mind wander. Eliminate distractions and create a soothing ambiance.

3. Embrace Mindfulness and Meditation:
- Practice a short mindfulness or meditation session to clear your mind. Focus on your breath and let go of immediate concerns.

4. Seek Unconventional Inspiration:
- Imagine yourself in an extraordinary, even otherworldly scenario. Picture yourself in a cosmic landscape or another realm where the rules of reality don't apply.

> "Inspiration knows no boundaries and often emerges from the enigmatic and unknown corners of our existence."

5. Visualize Encounter with Cosmic Entities:
- In your mind's eye, envision meeting beings from beyond our world. Imagine them sharing cryptic insights or gifts of wisdom. What do they offer to assist you in your endeavor?

6. Absorb Cosmic Inspiration:
- Allow yourself to absorb this cosmic wisdom and let it influence your thinking. Embrace the feeling of wonder, awe, and boundless creativity.

7. Record Ideas and Solutions:
- Immediately after your cosmic encounter visualization, jot down any brilliant ideas or solutions that come to mind. Capture them in a notebook, digital document, or your preferred note-taking method.

8. Analyze and Apply Insights:
- Review the ideas you've recorded and assess their potential in solving your real-world challenge. Are there innovative solutions or fresh perspectives among them?

9. Experiment and Implement:
- Act on the insights gained from your cosmic encounter. Experiment with new approaches to address your problem and observe the results.

10. Reflect and Adapt:
- After applying cosmic-inspired solutions, take time to reflect on their effectiveness. Adjust your approach as needed and refine your strategies.

11. Share Your Experience:
- Consider sharing your cosmic-inspired journey and any remarkable outcomes with friends, colleagues, or an online community. Inspire others to think outside the box as well.

By opening your mind to unconventional sources of inspiration, you can access a wellspring of creativity and innovative thinking, just as Mr. Grant Money did during his cosmic revelation. Remember that inspiration can strike in the most unexpected places, and embracing the unknown can lead to groundbreaking solutions.

Discussion Questions

1. The story of Mr. Grant Money's cosmic encounter highlights the concept of inspiration striking unexpectedly and innovation arising from embracing the unknown. How can individuals and organizations foster a creative and innovative mindset in their grant acquisition efforts?

2. Mr. Grant Money chose to keep his special power and encounter with beings of higher intelligence a secret, sharing it only through tales in his journal. What are the potential benefits and drawbacks of sharing unconventional sources of inspiration or unique experiences in the field of grant acquisition or philanthropy?

3. The story touches on the idea that innovative solutions and breakthroughs often come from unexpected sources or experiences. Can you think of other instances in the world of grant acquisition where unconventional inspiration or encounters have led to remarkable outcomes? What lessons can be drawn from these experiences that may be applicable to the broader field of grant acquisition?

4. The narrative suggests that Mr. Grant Money's cosmic encounter provided him with a well of inspiration. How can individuals and organizations maintain a consistent source of inspiration and innovation in their grant acquisition efforts? Are there strategies or practices that can help cultivate creativity and open-mindedness in the grant application process?

5. Mr. Grant Money's cosmic encounter was a surreal and extraordinary experience that had a profound impact on his grant acquisition abilities. Do you believe that unconventional experiences or sources of inspiration can be harnessed effectively in the professional world of grants and philanthropy? What might be the role of creativity and unique perspectives in addressing complex social and environmental challenges through grant funding?

 Big Idea "Cosmic Idea Exploration Journal"

Develop a specialized journal or digital tool designed to encourage individuals to document their most creative and unconventional ideas. This journal can include prompts, inspirational quotes, and exercises aimed at pushing the boundaries of traditional thinking. It's a space where users can embrace the unknown and capture those sparks of brilliance that often arise unexpectedly. Over time, it can become a valuable resource for personal or professional development, fostering a culture of innovation.

🔍 Word Search

Join Mr. Grant Money on a journey that transcends the ordinary in the bustling city of London. In this word search puzzle, discover 14 words related to his extraordinary encounter with cosmic beings, inspiration, and innovation that propel his grant acquisition prowess to new heights.

In this puzzle, discover the words related to the extraordinary adventures of Mr. Grant Money. Can you find all the hidden words that capture the essence of this remarkable story?

Now, here are the 14 words for the word search puzzle based on the story:

C	C	E	S	C	E	P	T	E	R	O	M	U	E
I	J	C	L	P	N	I	N	C	P	E	T	N	C
P	N	A	O	B	G	P	S	T	R	B	O	T	E
O	O	N	I	I	A	N	E	U	T	D	A	N	T
R	N	T	O	N	B	C	S	E	N	N	C	T	O
H	S	I	R	V	S	C	C	O	P	C	Q	S	J
T	N	C	G	E	A	P	L	E	O	N	U	E	O
N	O	M	R	U	A	T	I	I	P	E	I	C	U
A	I	C	A	N	A	S	I	R	S	M	S	R	R
L	T	I	N	T	I	A	U	O	A	I	I	E	N
I	U	M	T	I	T	T	U	R	N	T	T	A	
H	L	S	C	N	D	T	I	H	E	C	I	C	L
P	O	O	O	R	E	N	N	C	E	D	O	O	O
C	S	C	O	R	E	T	N	U	O	C	N	E	N

PHILANTHROPIC
COSMIC
INSPIRATION
SOLUTIONS
TREASURED
GRANT
ACQUISITION
ENCOUNTER
SECRET
SCEPTER
INNOVATION
JOURNAL
LONDON
IMPECCABLE

"The beauty of our world lies in its ability to surprise and astound, to reveal untold mysteries just beyond the veil of the familiar. Embrace the enigmatic, for within it lies the wellspring of limitless inspiration."

AFTERWARD

Congratulations, dear readers, on completing another thrilling volume of Mr. Grant Money's extraordinary adventures. As you reach the end of "Grantopoly," we hope you find yourself inspired, motivated, and ready to take on the world of grant acquisition with newfound wisdom and determination.

Throughout this volume, you've witnessed Mr. Grant Money's ingenuity, resilience, and unwavering commitment to success. These stories have illustrated that, indeed, nothing can stop a person who has set their mind on victory, no matter the hurdles they face.

Our hope is that these adventures have sparked your own determination and resolve. As you reflect on the lessons you've learned in these pages, consider how they can be applied to your own grant acquisition journey. Remember that it's not just about reading the stories but implementing the strategies, engaging in the exercises, and internalizing the wisdom imparted by Mr. Grant Money.

Your journey in the world of grants has likely had its challenges and triumphs, and this volume has equipped you with valuable insights to navigate the ever-evolving landscape of grant acquisition. The lessons here transcend the stories themselves, offering you an opportunity to elevate your understanding, skills, and potential.

As you continue your journey from one challenge to the next, we encourage you to explore the next series of adventures in Volumes 4 and 5. Mr. Grant Money's tales will continue to inspire and educate you, pushing the boundaries of what's possible in grant acquisition. Each new adventure will grant you the privilege of accompanying Mr. Grant Money on remarkable journeys that tap into his well of experience, creativity, and wisdom.

To further support your growth in the realm of grant acquisition, we invite you to explore other valuable resources offered by Mr. Grant Money at GrantCentralUSA.com. You'll find two-day grant training sessions, a wealth of information in our podcast, and insightful blog posts. For personalized guidance and consultations, visit GrantAcquisition.com. Don't forget to check out GrantWriterStore.com for stylish apparel that can help you stand out as you embark on your grant acquisition journey.

Remember that nothing can stop you when you've made up your mind to win. Continue to push the boundaries of your understanding, explore new avenues, and relentlessly pursue your grant acquisition goals. Mr. Grant Money's adventures have proven that the sky's the limit, and your grant success awaits.

In the words of the great Arthur Ashe, "Start where you are. Use what you have. Do what you can." Your journey may have started with Volume 1, but each volume you complete brings you closer to becoming the grant acquisition expert you aspire to be. Keep moving forward, and your adventures have only just begun.

ABOUT THE AUTHOR

Rodney Walker is a man on a mission. He's dedicated his life to helping others secure funding for their projects and dreams. As the President of Grant Central USA, a grant development training firm internationally known for helping organizations land six-figure and seven-figure grants and shave months off the time it takes to get funded, Rodney has helped clients raise over half a billion dollars in grants!

He's also an author of numerous books, online courses and the founder of two popular grant writing conferences: The Education Grants Conference and First Responders Grants Conference. Grant Central USA has also partnered with several universities, including Regis University, Hawaii University, Oklahoma University, National University, Cal Poly University, and Florida Atlantic University.

Rodney is even the host of four podcasts: Get Funded with Rodney, Grant Writing Today, Grant Business Show, and Schools Winning Grants. He oversees Grant Success Advisors, an elite network of approved licensees who deliver today's leading training in grant development systems.

He has an extensive network of high-level contacts, including his Grant Writers Association group on LinkedIn with over 15,000+ members.

Considered a national authority in the grant industry, Grant Central USA's clients have included, The Magic Johnson Foundation, the George W. Bush Foundation, Ben Guillory and Danny Glover of the Robey Theatre Company, Hawaii State Teachers Association, United Way, Habitat for Humanity, and numerous school districts and city governments.

Rodney has produced over 730 videos on grant development on his popular YouTube channel and has taught over 240,000 people how to improve their grant writing efforts. "We have been helping our clients successfully get funded and launch new careers in grant writing since 2006 across the U.S. and worldwide, giving them both the competence and the confidence to win the grants at a high level."

He says his primary specialty is "Getting our clients funded with six-figure and seven-figure grants while helping grant professionals get paid what they are worth!"

In addition to his leadership experience at Grant Central USA, he has years of experience in Business and Professional Development in various sectors. He has been a sought-after expert in grant professional development, coaching, and the law of success.

As a media personality, he has interviewed numerous celebrities, including Snoop Dogg, Heisman Trophy Winners: Reggie Bush, Charles Woodson, Professional Boxer Laila Ali, America's Next Top Model Season 19 Winner: Laura James, NBA Champions: Draymond Green, Matt Barnes, National College Football Champions: Coach Mack Brown, and Vince Young, and countless others.

It's safe to say that Rodney knows his stuff regarding grants and working with champions!

GRANT MONEY MAGNET™

I am the Grant Money Magnet™, a relentless force that navigates the intricate maze of grant acquisition with unwavering determination and a strategic mind. Challenges are not obstacles; they are opportunities waiting to be seized. With every hurdle, I rise, armed with innovative solutions, pushing the boundaries of what's possible. My curiosity is my compass, guiding me through the maze of grant landscapes, uncovering hidden opportunities and transforming challenges into triumphs.

In the realm of grant development campaigns, I am the orchestrator of a symphony that goes beyond the basics of mere grant writing. My daily actions are a testament to my commitment, with well-defined grant goals propelling me forward. I am not a lone warrior; I am part of a powerful grant team, where collaboration amplifies our impact. Together, we transcend the ordinary, transforming aspirations into tangible results.

Grant funding doesn't elude me; I attract it with an irresistible magnetic force. My mind is a powerhouse of ideas, a generator of solutions that resonate with the aspirations of benefactors and the needs of society. Relentlessness is my mantra; there's no door I can't open, no avenue left unexplored. I don't just pursue grants; I nurture relationships, cultivating a network of allies who share my passion for impact. In my grant pursuit, I don't just raise funds; I raise friends and partners, forging alliances that extend beyond transactions into enduring collaborations.

As the architect of my grant destiny, I recognize that true power lies not just in acquiring funds but in the collective strength of a united effort. I am not merely a seeker of grants; I am a catalyst for transformative change. With each campaign, I etch my mark on the maze of philanthropy, weaving a narrative of impact that transcends the ordinary. Together with my grant team, I shape a future where challenges bow before innovation, and the resonance of our collaborative endeavors echoes through the corridors of progress. Grant by grant, we sculpt a legacy that stands as a testament to the limitless potential of unified action and unwavering dedication.

Recite and embrace the power of this statement daily; let its resonance shape your mindset and fuel your unwavering commitment to grant success.

GRANTOPOLY ROYAL RULES

Dive into a realm of funding mastery with Mr. Grant Money's 10 Grantopoly Royal Rules For Engagement - your strategic guide to securing maximum funding for your organization. Revisit these rules often and witness your grant success soar as you put them into practice! 🚀 💲 #GrantMastery #FundingSuccess

1. 🎯 **Master the Mission:** Clearly articulate your organization's mission in every proposal, demonstrating an unwavering commitment to your cause.

2. 🌟 **Impact is King:** Highlight the tangible, life-changing impact of your projects; grantors want to see real results.

3. 🤝 **Build Strategic Alliances:** Showcase partnerships with other organizations to demonstrate a united front in achieving common goals.

4. 📊 **Data Speaks Louder:** Back your proposals with compelling data and statistics that underscore the urgency and necessity of your work.

5. 📖 **Storytelling Magic:** Craft narratives that evoke empathy, connecting the funder emotionally to your mission and beneficiaries.

6. 💰 **Budget Brilliance:** Develop meticulously detailed budgets that align with project goals and ensure every dollar is well-spent.

7. 📈 **Transparent Metrics:** Articulate clear and measurable outcomes, outlining how the funding will drive positive change.

8. 🌐 **Engage the Community:** Illustrate strong community involvement and support, reflecting a broad network invested in your success.

9. 🔄 **Continuous Learning:** Demonstrate a commitment to improvement through feedback loops and adaptive strategies.

10. 🙏 **Express Gratitude:** Always express sincere gratitude for the grantor's consideration, building a foundation for long-term partnerships.

MR. GRANT MONEY'S IDIOMS

Welcome to a world of financial creativity and linguistic flair! In this collection, you'll find ten unique "Mr. Grant Money" idioms crafted to add a touch of wit and imagination to your discussions about grants and funding opportunities. These idioms are not just expressions; they're windows into the dynamic and often challenging realm of grant acquisition. Enjoy more of these with new ones in the next volumes.

1. Counting Mr. Grant's blessings:
Meaning: Refers to someone who is fortunate or financially well-off due to receiving a grant or unexpected financial assistance.

2. Chasing the Grant Dragon:
Meaning: Engaging in relentless pursuit of financial opportunities, especially grants, with uncertain outcomes.

3. Granting Wishes on a Shoestring:
Meaning: Achieving desired outcomes with limited financial resources, often through strategic grant utilization.

4. The Grant Rainmaker:
Meaning: A person or entity that consistently attracts grants and financial support, seemingly effortlessly.

5. Counting Grant Sheep:
Meaning: Having difficulty falling asleep due to financial worries, especially related to grant funding and resources.

6. Dancing for Grant Gold:
Meaning: Putting in extraordinary effort or going to great lengths to secure grant funding.

7. Granting the Goose that Lays Golden Eggs:
Meaning: Successfully managing and preserving a valuable source of ongoing grant income.

8. Caught in the Grant Web:
Meaning: Facing complexities and challenges associated with managing multiple grant-funded projects.

9. The Grant Magician:
Meaning: An individual with exceptional skills in obtaining and managing grants, making the process seem magical.

10. Granting a Mountain out of a Molehill:
Meaning: Exaggerating the impact or significance of a grant, especially during discussions or presentations.

INFORMATIONAL INTERVIEW

Informational interviews are an excellent way to gain valuable insights and knowledge from experienced grant professionals and grant makers. By engaging in conversations with experts in the field, you can enhance your understanding, learn best practices, and foster your continuous growth and development in the world of grant funding.

Instructions:

1. **Identify Potential Interviewees:**
   - Create a list of grant professionals, grant makers, and other individuals with relevant insights whom you would like to interview. Consider factors such as expertise, experience, and industry focus.

2. **Reach Out:**
   - Craft a polite and concise email introducing yourself and explaining your interest in an informational interview. Request a convenient time for a meeting, either in person, over the phone, or via video call.

3. **Prepare Questions:**
   - Develop a list of thoughtful questions to guide your conversation. Tailor these questions to the individual's expertise and experiences. Be sure to ask about challenges they've faced, successes they've had, and advice they can offer.

4. **Schedule the Interview:**
   - Once you receive a positive response, schedule a time for the informational interview. Be respectful of their time and come prepared with your questions.

5. **Conduct the Interview:**
   - During the interview, actively listen, take notes, and ask follow-up questions. Be respectful of their time constraints and focus on extracting valuable insights.

6. **Reflect and Analyze:**
   - After each interview, take some time to reflect on the key takeaways. Consider how the information can be applied to your own work and goals.

7. **Thank You Note:**
   - Send a thank-you email expressing your gratitude for their time and insights. Mention specific points from the interview that were particularly helpful.

INFORMATIONAL INTERVIEW

Interviewee Information:

Name:
Title:
Organization:
Contact Information:
Date of Interview:

Interview Questions:

1. What led you to pursue a career in grant writing /management/grant making?
2. Can you share a significant challenge you faced in your career and how you overcame it?
3. What are the key skills and qualities you believe are crucial for success in this field?
4. How do you stay updated on the latest trends and changes in the grant industry?
5. Can you provide insights into your most successful grant project? What made it successful?
6. What advice do you have for someone looking to advance their career in grant management/grant making?
7. Are there any common misconceptions about working in grant-related roles that you'd like to address?

Key Takeaways:

Learnings:
Actionable Steps:
Connections Made:

Next Steps:

Identify Additional Contacts:
Schedule Next Informational Interview:
Implement Insights into Your Work:

This worksheet is designed to guide you through the process of conducting informational interviews and extracting valuable information to support your continuous growth and development in the field of grant funding. Good luck!

Take Your Grant Game To The Next Level With These...

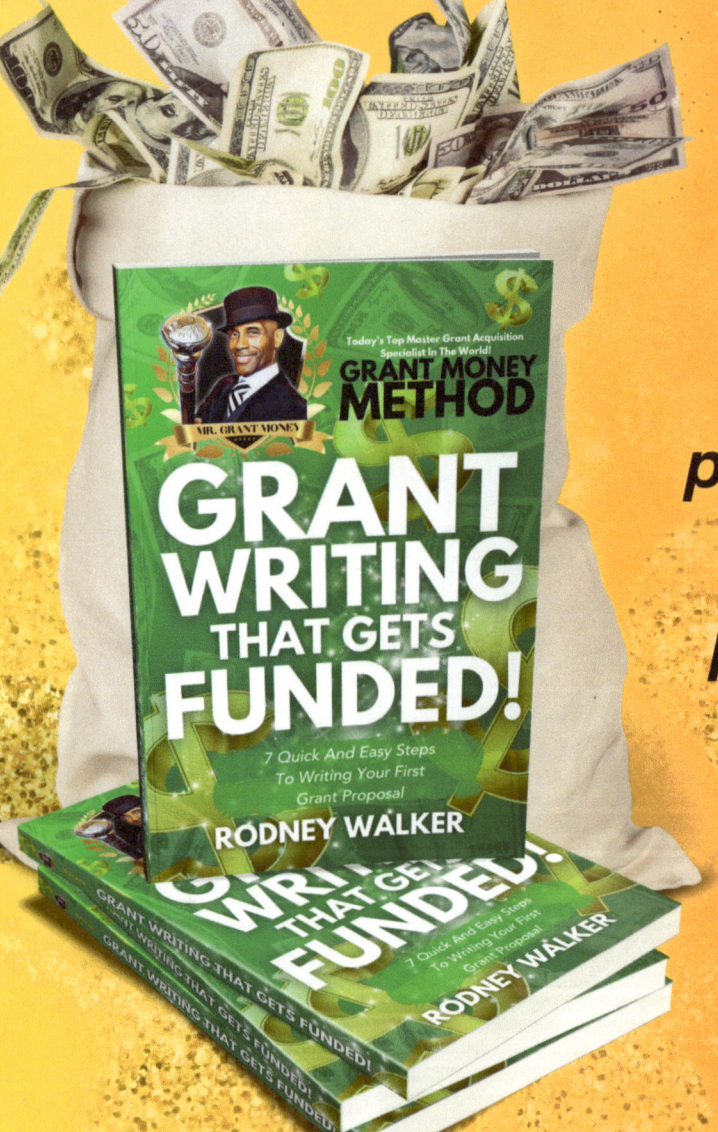

"Rodney is a grant genius! His courses are well thought out and clear, making the process of learning grant writing easier."
- Elena Esparza, Procurement/Contract Administrator

Transform your grant proposals into lucrative successes with my proven strategies that have raised millions.

"I hit my benchmark goal of $350,000.00!"
- Rebecca Laharia

"Thank you so much for your help. Probably not a day has gone by that I didn't use something."
- Evelyn Barker, Director of Grants and Special Project at University of Texas

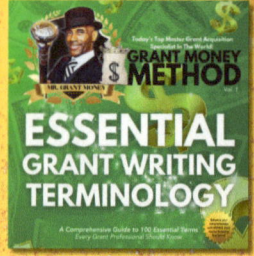   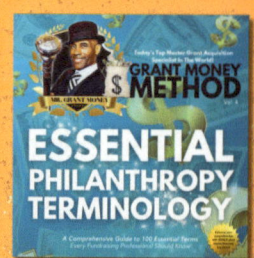 

Boost your confidence in grant writing, fundraising, and finance! Elevate your communication skills with the **Fundraising Fundamentals Vocabulary Builder Series** – *100 essential terms in each series.* Invest in knowledge, empower your success!

Enjoy More Amazing Adventures with Mr. Grant Money!

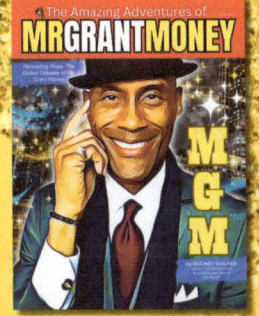
Harvesting Hope: The Global Odyssey of Mr. Grant Money
Vol. 1
ISBN 978-0-9659275-0-5

The Artful Navigator: Mr. Grant Money's Chronicles
Vol. 2
ISBN 978-0-9659275-2-9

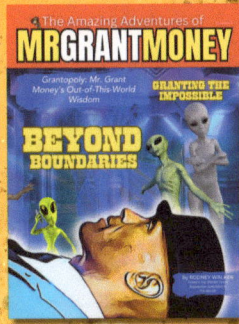
Grantopoly: Mr. Grant Money's Out-of-This-World Wisdom
Vol. 3
ISBN 978-0-9659275-3-6

Grant Odyssey: Mr. Grant Money's Time-Traveling Feats
Vol. 4
ISBN 978-0-9659275-4-3

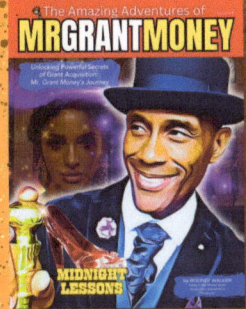
Unlocking Powerful Secrets of Grant Acquisition
Vol. 5
ISBN 978-0-9659275-5-0

Gain Exclusive Access To Companion Resources & Bonus Materials at MrGrantMoney.com and GrantCentralUsa.com

Bring the transformative Adventures and lessons of Mr. Grant Money to your educational institution or organization by **acquiring your license today**. Enjoy exclusive access to a wealth of online resources, such as special reports, worksheets, videos, audio training, discounts, and more, elevating the entire experience to the next level!

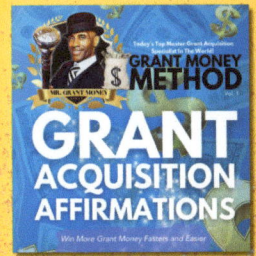
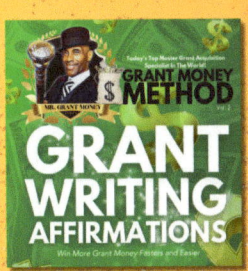

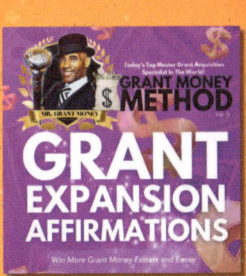

Envision and affirm your grant success in the same proactive spirit as Mr. Grant Money. **Experience the power of these daily affirmations** to inspire and motivate your journey toward success!

www.ingramcontent.com/pod-product-compliance
Lightning Source LLC
Chambersburg PA
CBHW041546220426
43665CB00002B/45